ACROSS A BRIDGE OF FIRE

An American Teen's Odyssey from the Burn Ward to the Edge of the Cambodian Killing Fields

SCOTT ALLEN

Across a Bridge of Fire: An American Teen's Odyssey from the Burn Ward to the Edge of the Cambodian Killing Fields
Copyright © 2024 Scott Allen

Produced and printed by Stillwater River Publications. All rights reserved. Written and produced in the United States of America. This book may not be reproduced or sold in any form without the expressed, written permission of the author(s) and publisher.

Visit our website at **www.StillwaterPress.com** for more information.

First Stillwater River Publications Edition.

ISBN: 978-1-963296-26-6 *(hardcover)*
ISBN: 978-1-963296-25-9 *(paperback)*

Library of Congress Control Number: 2024903003

1 2 3 4 5 6 7 8 9 10
Written by Scott Allen.
Cover design by Barbara Braman.
Interior book design by Matthew St. Jean.
Published by Stillwater River Publications, West Warwick, RI, USA.

Names: Allen, Scott (Scott Andrew), author.
Title: Across a bridge of fire : an American teen's odyssey from the burn ward to the edge of the Cambodian killing fields / Scott Allen.
Description: First Stillwater River Publications edition. | West Warwick, RI, USA : Stillwater River Publications, [2024]
Identifiers: ISBN: 978-1-963296-26-6 (hardcover) | 978-1-963296-25-9 (paperback) | LCCN: 2024903003
Subjects: LCSH: Allen, Scott (Scott Andrew)—Childhood and youth. | Burns and scalds—Patients—United States—Biography. | Teenagers—Wounds and injuries. | Humanitarian aid workers—Thailand—Biography. | Refugees—Cambodia—History—20th century. | Refugee camps—Thailand—History—20th century. | Genocide—Cambodia—History—20th century. | LCGFT: Autobiographies.
Classification: LCC: RD96.4 .A45 2024 | DDC: 617.11092—dc23

The views and opinions expressed in this book are solely those of the author(s) and do not necessarily reflect the views and opinions of the publisher.

PRAISE FOR *ACROSS A BRIDGE OF FIRE* BY SCOTT ALLEN

It was the psychological pain of facial burn scars that made a seemingly comfortable American life nearly unbearable. In escaping the comforts—and agony—of the life he knew, Dr. Allen describes how he stumbled upon what would ultimately become his mission: to do what he could to alleviate suffering. More than anything, this is a story of resilience. While Dr. Allen never succeeded at outrunning his pain, the way he learned to cope with it, and what he's done with his life since, is magnificent. Five stars!

**GERRI SHAFTEL CONSTANT,
PRODUCER, 17-TIME EMMY AWARD WINNER,
CBS NEWS & STATIONS LOS ANGELES**

Scott Allen's *Across a Bridge of Fire* is a memoir that takes us into the most difficult circumstances and still finds a way forward all the while questioning what it means to be human. From childhood trauma survivor to compassionate professional, Dr. Allen searches for the purpose to contribute to positive change.

**PAMELA YATES, SUNDANCE SPECIAL JURY PRIZE WINNING
DOCUMENTARY FILM DIRECTOR AND HUMAN RIGHTS ACTIVIST**

Scott was the youngest caseworker I hired during my 16-year tenure with the Joint Voluntary Agency team attached to the Refugee Section of the US Embassy. He would subsequently prove to be among the very best. His tale of pursuing life's purpose among refugees both in Thailand and the US is nothing less than a gift to dreamers of all ages.

**DENNIS GRACE, FORMER DIRECTOR OF THE JOINT VOLUNTARY
AGENCY IN THAILAND, AND SPECIAL ASSISTANT TO THE
PRESIDENT IN THE OFFICE OF FAITH-BASED AND COMMUNITY
INITIATIVES UNDER PRESIDENT GEORGE W. BUSH**

Dr. Scott A. Allen has written a true masterpiece, describing the challenges and adventures of his youth that were formative and led to him being a true leader, advocate, and successful champion for the least fortunate among us. His journey spans an idyllic childhood to surviving as a patient in a terrifying pediatric burn unit to working in a border refugee camp and documenting the horrors of the killing fields from those who survived it, to the heights of academia and international human rights advocacy.

JODY RICH, MD, PROFESSOR OF MEDICINE, FOUNDER OF THE CENTER FOR HEALTH AND JUSTICE TRANSFORMATION, BROWN UNIVERSITY

Scott Allen has dedicated his life to offering not only compassionate, expert medical care to some of the most vulnerable and shunned people in society—the disabled, prisoners, and immigrants—but also his voice as an advocate and truth-teller. Through Allen's moving and vivid excavation of how a horrific early tragedy set him on a path of service and incredible adventure, we understand how his mind, heart, and life were inevitably forged to do such good for so many, choosing moral courage and compassion at every turn.

DANA GOLD, SENIOR COUNSEL, GOVERNMENT ACCOUNTABILITY PROJECT

Brilliant and courageous. Scott Allen digs into his own soul, confronts his own pain, and finds the resources needed to help others who are struggling. A needed look into a very difficult piece of history—the Cambodian refugees in Thailand, one of the more distal impacts of our war in Vietnam—and finds dignity in the work of international aid, however fraught. An important reflection in a time of too many wars and far too many refugees. When the work of each person matters, in the face of our collective failure to prevent these endless wars from occurring.

MICHAEL FINE, MD, COMMUNITY ORGANIZER AND AUTHOR OF *ABUNDANCE*

In today's polarized, warring world, we often wonder whether there is any idealism left. Here is a memoir from another painful era of one young man's courage to live his dream of helping war-ravaged people heal their trauma while also healing his own. This rivetingly emotional story will leave no reader unchanged. It holds out the hope that idealism is not dead, but rather waiting to be born in the hearts of all who refuse to give in to cynicism and despair.

EVAN HOWARD, AUTHOR OF *THE GALILEAN SECRET*

Scott Allen is among those whose lives can inspire hope in people seeking direction to navigate our troubled times. In *Across a Bridge of Fire*, he tells us of his lifelong struggle to transform horror and suffering into compassion and caring. The story is captivating, and the message is much needed in contemporary America.

**STEPHEN SOLDZ, PROFESSOR,
BOSTON GRADUATE SCHOOL OF PSYCHOANALYSIS;
CO-FOUNDER, COALITION FOR AN ETHICAL PSYCHOLOGY**

As an 85% burn survivor, I can attest that being burned is the most devastating injury known to man. A burn of Scott's degree tested his mind, body, and soul. Through adversity he was introduced to himself. A truly healing and inspirational chronicle.

**GEORGE E. PESSOTTI, PRESIDENT EMERITUS, BURN SURVIVORS
OF NEW ENGLAND; AUTHOR OF *REASON FOR LIVING: A BURN
SURVIVOR'S STORY OF HOPE AND REBIRTH***

Scott Allen's unique voice is a welcome addition to the modern history of Southeast Asia.

**ELIZABETH BECKER, FORMER *WASHINGTON POST* CAMBODIA
WAR CORRESPONDENT; AWARD-WINNING NPR SENIOR FOREIGN
EDITOR AND *NEW YORK TIMES* CORRESPONDENT; AUTHOR OF
WHEN THE WAR WAS OVER AND *YOU DON'T BELONG HERE***

I'm not telling you to make the world better, because I don't think that progress is necessarily part of the package. I'm just telling you to live in it. Not just to endure it, not just to suffer it, not just to pass through it, but to live in it. To look at it. To try to get the picture. To live recklessly. To take chances. To make your own work and take pride in it. To seize the moment.

Joan Didion,
University of California Riverside
1975 commencement address

Across a Bridge of Fire

THE LETTER

March 4, 1980

Dear Mom and Dad,

I have left for Thailand. I'm sorry I had to leave this way, but it is the only way. And believe me, leaving without telling you is one of the largest burdens that I will carry with me. But, as I said, it is the only way.

Whatever consolation it is, I am comforted by the fact that I discussed my plans at great length with both of you. Individually. You know my motives about as well as you ever will. I was able to hear your ideas, opinions, and advice. I did listen.

But, unfortunately, as my parents, you couldn't let me embark on my proposed travels without being accompanied by a specific relief organization. I respect this decision. Had I been in your position, I would have had no choice but to make the decision you had to, and did, make.

I have been researching my plans for approximately the past ten months. In the process, I talked with many people from the United Nations, International Red Cross, Peace Corps, and the Royal Thai Embassy. I had come to the conclusion that even if I could cut through the red tape, I would not be able to go for about a year. I also have been told by many sources that there is a need for people in the camps.

I ask that you only accept one thing. You are not morally responsible for my actions. Had you been able to stop me, I would have found another way. I was determined to go, and I feel strongly that I have made the right decision.

Before you panic, there are a lot of details that you don't know yet. They are the details of transportation, vaccinations, and relief agencies.

Visa and Passport: I have been issued a United States passport and I also have been granted a nonimmigrant visa which is extendible.

Transportation: This morning (Wednesday, March 5, 1980) I took a Greyhound bus from Hartford to JFK Airport. There, I caught a Pan American flight to Bangkok, Thailand with stops in Tokyo and Hong Kong. The cost was $550. Buses run from Bangkok to Sakeo camp, east of Bangkok.

Vaccinations and Health Statement: I was vaccinated in Hartford against Yellow Fever. I am also carrying a World Health Organization Vaccination Record I obtained from the state health department. I also have a letter from Dr. Dutton stating that the smallpox immunization is unnecessary for my proposed travels. It also states that I am in good health.

Money, Food and Baggage: I am carrying with me $100 in traveler's checks. I will also be refunded two hundred dollars for a commercial flight from Bangkok to Hong Kong that I have booked and will cancel. I needed this ticket in order to be granted a visa. I also have about a week's worth of dehydrated and canned food. I have a canteen and forty gallons worth of water disinfectant tablets. I have a backpack, clothes, sleeping bag, two ground cloths, and many other miscellaneous survival materials.

Relief Agencies in Thailand: About one week ago, I talked on the phone for the third time with Pat Pickering at the Peace Corps in Washington, D.C. She is the National Coordinator for Volunteers for the Cambodian relief effort for the Peace Corps. I outlined my plan to go to Thailand, and she was supportive, but she explained that the Peace Corps was not likely to accept someone my age. She also explained that once a Peace Corps member is accepted, they are turned over to the UN in Geneva and there was no guarantee that I'd be assigned to the Cambodian border. She didn't know the names of anyone in charge. However, she did know that many more volunteers were needed.

So, I took her information about the UN and after many calls I ended up talking to a Mr. Leen of the High Commissioner for Refugees, UN, Geneva. I explained my situation and asked him if he could give me any direction in the way of names. Well, he said there were hundreds of agencies over there, but he gave me information on eight of the larger English-speaking ones located in Bangkok.

For each of the following organizations, I have the name of the person in charge, their address in Bangkok, and their telephone number. They are:

>   Save the Children Fund
>   International Rescue Committee
>   World Vision Foundation
>   YMCA
>   CAMA Services
>   Church of Christ in Thailand
>   Catholic Relief Services
>   Food for the Hungry, International

School: As far as school is concerned, I only need one English credit to graduate. I discussed in confidence my plans with Mr. Boldway, who said that if I kept a journal, he would give me school credit. I have left Mr. Salvatore a letter informing him that I have dropped Physics and Calculus and accept the "F"s.

I have left the college matter untouched. I have submitted my applications to Harvard and Bates. When I get a job in Thailand, and if I get accepted at either school, I will ask for a deferral for admissions.

Above all, I realize that I have hurt you. I am sorry. As for forgiving me, that is something you may never choose to do.

I have quite a challenging road ahead of me. And even though you are not responsible for any danger I may place myself in, I *must give you credit for any successes that I may have in Thailand. For, even in this time of separation, I still am, and always will be, your son.*

I hope you will be strong, as I must be. Accept what is as what is.

I will contact you as soon as possible. My first stop in Bangkok is the American Embassy.

Until then.

Love, Scott

In March 1980, at the age of seventeen, I quietly slipped away from the security and comfort of white middle-class New England suburbia and boarded a plane bound for Thailand with a plan to reach the Cambodian border in my effort to respond to the unfolding refugee crisis there. I was heading for the Cambodian border to do whatever I could to respond to the scenes of desperate and starving refugees that had filled the international news coverage in the fall of 1979. Despite having researched as best I could with limited resources, I had absolutely no idea what I would find there.

Yet I felt compelled to embark on this mission. I felt deeply in my soul it was the right thing to do. In some fundamental way, I felt like I had no choice, that once I made the decision to go, I could not have stopped myself even if I tried.

I'm not sure that I even understood what motivated me. Maybe I was searching for other people who knew what I knew about human suffering. Maybe those people would understand me.

Maybe I just wanted to do something to respond to an internal turmoil I could no longer ignore.

THE PUNISHMENT

July 1980, Thailand

"Your mother and I have decided that we will not punish you for what you did," my father said to me four months later when he and my mom came to visit me in Thailand.

"What you have done has its own punishment. For the rest of your life, you will have to explain what you did and why you did it to everyone who asks."

"Oh, and just a heads-up—everyone will ask."

The truth is, I don't really know why I did what I did. But it all starts with a fire.

THE ACCIDENT

I do not tell this story. Ever. I keep it in the box that I almost never open. I will only tell it once and only because to tell the bigger story, I need to first tell this story.

There was a small clearing in the lush, wooded forest surrounding my childhood home in northwestern Connecticut. Something happened in that clearing.

To begin with, there is the fact that volatile fumes that waft from an open container can ignite into a fireball. In the summer of 1972, I did not know this when I suggested to my brother that we use gasoline to help us light a campfire. I was ten; my brother Bruce was eleven. Although he was the elder, I was quite precocious in my ability to come up with stupid ideas. I often took the lead in the many mistakes we made together. This time was no exception. It was my bright idea. And I thought my idea was great.

We would pour gasoline over a rock and light it on fire.

The fire lit effortlessly.

I felt heat on my foot. I looked down and saw a small area on the top of my right black Converse high-top sneaker on fire. As I bent down to remove the shoe, there was a whooshing roar. And then...

AND THEN I CANNOT CONNECT the piece of my life up to this point with everything that came after. Nothing connects before and after. I do not know where I went. I do not know what happened. There was no time. There was nothingness. I was gone.

AND THEN I WAS BACK. Flames engulfed me. In the horror of the moment, my face and body burning, I thought I had already died. It may have been seconds or minutes, days or years, I can't say, but it is a moment, and it all comes down to this moment when everything changed.

Then, in the next suspended, free-floating expanse of time while I burned, the pain went away. I was no longer in my own body but was somehow above it. Above and to the left. In a moment detached from time or space, I mourned my own death. It saddened me to realize that I was just the dumb kid who played with matches and died. That was it. That was all my life was. A waste.

I let go. I felt peace.

More seconds or days or years passed, and the pain returned as I returned to my body. I was still alive. And I was still burning. "Drop and roll, drop and roll," the firefighter at school had taught us. I fell to the ground.

After awkward fits and rolls, I emerged from the fire. I patted the last flames from my arms and legs, the skin already peeling away. For the first time, I became aware of my environment. My brother and a friend, John, had been missed by the fireball and were shouting and screaming in complete shock and confusion. John was stamping out the remaining flames on the ground with his bare feet. With his *bare feet*.

Then quiet. The ground. The trees. The sky. The air that I breathed. My hand. Look at my hand. My God, look at my hand. That can't be my hand.

I felt lightheaded.

I was back.
But everything had changed.

THE NEXT THING I REMEMBER, the three of us were stumbling in a daze over the gravel driveway toward my house. We remained at some distance from one another as we staggered towards the front door.

I raised my left hand to feel my shirt. It was gone. I reached toward my stinging back. My right arm looked like hard yellow leather and was already peeling. The smell of burnt hair and skin filled the air.

"Am I still burning?" I shouted.

No answer.

"Am I still burning?!"

"No," replied my brother. He was crying.

In the clearing of our driveway turnaround, the sky looked so blue. Not blue like before. A different blue. Everything was different.

THROUGH THE FRONT DOOR. I needed to make it to the stairs past my mother. I just needed to make it to my room. To buy time. To figure out what just happened.

There was my mother. At the bottom of the stairs in the kitchen. She had a terrified look on her face.

"What happened to you?"

Louder. "What happened to you?!!"

I don't remember much after that, but eventually, Mrs. Anderson, our next-door neighbor, arrived. I was placed in the yellow wicker rocking chair in the kitchen. My mother was on the phone with the doctor, having already called the fire and rescue. But we lived in a remote wooded area of town. It would be time before they arrived. Sheets were put over me. Water was poured over me from a watering can.

We were getting water all over the kitchen floor.

I heard sirens in the distance, but the volunteer firefighters couldn't find our house. Mom helped me to the back seat of our car, and I laid down across the rear bench seat. The numbness was now gone, the pain in my face, right arm, back and legs was stinging and all-consuming. I was feeling faint. I closed my eyes.

As we drove the twenty minutes to the hospital, my mother stopped only briefly to flag down a lost fire truck and inform them that the fire was out and that she was taking me to the hospital. Minutes from the small local hospital in Winsted, she pulled over in front of the community college where my father taught.

He opened the rear door and peered in with me. Calm. In control. Without a word, he closed the rear door. My mother slid over on the front bench seat and dad took the wheel of the car for the final short drive to the hospital.

At the hospital, they were expecting me. There were many nurses and aides for this small two-room emergency unit.

I was placed in the same green tiled room I had been in several years earlier when I required stitches for a facial laceration. Same white cabinets with glass doors. Black gurneys. White sheets. Black tile floor. They had given me a box of raisins for being so brave and holding still during the suturing the last time I was here. Would I get raisins again?

Again, I was outside my body. Above and to the left.

Doctors and nurses swirled around me in a curious dance. My mom and dad stood behind them.

A nurse told me, "You're going to feel a pinprick."

Within a minute, the noise dampened. I felt calmer and my mind became foggy.

A lean, quick man with wire-rimmed glasses wearing a long open white coat and surgical scrubs entered the room. He calmly took control and issued orders to the nurses. My shorts and burnt Converse sneakers were cut away from my body with large scissors. Dr. Dutton, the surgeon, turned to my parents.

"I think he'll survive," he said. "But we need to take him directly to the operating room."

Moments later, we were at the operating room's double doors. In the chaos, the nurses couldn't find an IV stand, so my father was standing at the edge of the gurney, holding a bottle of IV fluids above me. I looked up at him.

Everything will be fine he said. I trusted my dad. I didn't feel scared anymore. I closed my eyes and sank into the nothingness.

THE HOSPITAL

The three months that followed the gas can explosion were a journey through seemingly endless hours of physical pain, fixation on my next narcotic shot, and confinement in a hospital bed. And in between the painful dressing changes and treatment, there also was plenty of time for boredom.

Burns covered over a third of my body. The entire right side of my face, my right arm, right leg, small areas on my left leg, arm, and the right half of my back were involved. My right hand suffered the worst damage. My fingers had burned down to the bone and the tendons that raise the fingers and many of the joints were totally destroyed. The surgical removal of dead tissue performed urgently in the operating room left gaping wounds that would take months to heal. The treatment involved daily whirlpool baths followed by the application of a stinging white antiseptic cream called *Sulfamylon* but known to patients as "white lightning," frequent returns to the operating room for further removal of dead skin and muscle—debridement—and eventually skin grafts to speed the healing of the most deeply burned areas of my body including my right arm and leg…and time.

Many people were nice enough to visit me across that long

summer in my local hospital. My parents both worked during the day, so visits from family, friends, and neighbors were a welcome diversion from the pain and tedium. At various times, family friends who knew I loved music came to play guitar for me, and it made a huge impression. Music always made me feel better.

But not all visitors were helpful. One day, as I lay on my bed, I was drawn out of my daydreaming by the sound of someone at my door clucking, "Tsk, tsk, tsk."

I looked over where, to my utter horror, two old women stood who I had hoped to never see again: my former fourth-grade teacher, Mrs. Gleszer, and her colleague, Mrs. Wilder.

"Oh, my," added Mrs. Wilder as they shook their heads and frowned.

"You know I told you not to play with matches," Mrs. Gleszer admonished.

To the best of my memory, she never said any such thing.

Mrs. Gleszer was a hideous creature to me. She had a mean curve of her upper spine that resulted in her head emerging from the middle of her chest. Her lipstick was always applied slightly off target, creating the appearance of two mouths—the anatomic one and the artistic one, as if she were a living Picasso.

She considered herself a gifted artist and was known for displaying her own pen and ink drawings from the walls on parent-teacher night instead of student works.

I hated Mrs. Gleszer.

It was the early 1970s and my parents allowed my brother and me to grow our hair long. Mrs. Gleszer viewed this as a threat to classroom order and at one point called me up to the front of the class to make fun of my "girlish" hair. For dramatic effect, she pulled a pair of paper scissors from her desk drawer and snipped a bit of my hair. I responded by kicking her in her shin. My father had to be called from work to collect me from the principal's office. Dad was sympathetic, but still rebuked me for my response.

"Scott, she was in the wrong, but you shouldn't have kicked her."

Mrs. Gleszer loomed over me judgmentally as I lay in my hospital bed, shaking her head in disapproval. I suppressed an urge to kick her again. I didn't have the strength.

Having administered her lesson, she departed, leaving me with the gift of a stale box of chocolates, with several pieces missing. I was rescued by my nurse, who arrived and gave me a much-needed Demerol shot.

I quickly learned to love Demerol. It was like magic. Not only did it numb the excruciating pain of wound debridement, dressing changes, and the sting of *Sulfamylon* cream, it calmed me and made me euphoric. It made every dark thought in my brain disappear. For a short but lovely period after each shot, the world was a wonderful place. I was on a cloud where everything was peaceful, soft, and lovely. Demerol was the best thing in the world! Except it didn't last. The relief was always too short. I hated coming down off a high. I grew increasingly desperate for the next shot. I knew the schedule for when I could ask for another dose. I always pushed the nurse call button early.

Time passed slowly. I simply did what I needed to do. At ten, I viewed the situation in very concrete terms. I simply put one foot in front of the other (figuratively, as I was bed bound) and did what I needed to do to get through, minute by minute. Physical pain was consuming, but I only focused on surviving that moment until the pain was relieved or subsided. I was not mature or developed enough to process the emotional trauma. The near-death experience. The slowly passing hours looking through the open window at the trees outside and up towards the treetops on the hill. The bite of the *Sulfamylon* and raw pain dressing changes. The comfort of narcotics and the discomfort of their eventual withdrawal. I survived these days in simple ways. I did not reflect. I was often alone at night in the odd solitary world of a child in a hospital. I was certain I heard angels singing to me one night, and I did not find it odd. I have never heard them since.

It filled me with pride when my paternal grandfather Grampi, a veteran of over three devastating years in the South Pacific, gave me his own wooden plaque with his PT Boat Squadron #25 insignia.

"I carried this with me throughout the war in the South Pacific.

I want you to have it. You have been as brave as any sailor or soldier I served with," he said as he presented me with the plaque as I lay in my hospital bed.

I was stunned that he would give me something he carried in the war.

He said I was brave. I was not brave. I feared every dressing change.

I also felt powerless. Totally controlled by others. If I could have run away from it all, I would have. I only pushed on through because I had no choice.

I had been hospitalized at a small local community hospital in northwestern Connecticut for the first few months following my injury under the care of Dr. Dutton, a general surgeon who had just returned from a tour of duty caring for burned soldiers in Vietnam. I was often in tremendous physical pain and the most severely injured child there, so I received extra attention. The supportive environment of a small community hospital was reassuring. It was summer, and as there was no air conditioning, my windows were always open, and as the hospital was set high on a hill, there was often a refreshing breeze. I had a little black-and-white hospital TV that got only two channels clearly, but I could leave it on all night, and no one ever said anything. I couldn't do that at home.

After two months under Dr. Dutton's care, having undergone extensive debridement of burned tissue followed by skin grafts from my thighs to my right arm and leg and my back, I was transferred to the Boston Shriners Burn Institute for Children for expert consultation and perhaps further orthopedic hand surgery or plastic surgery for scar reduction.

At Shriners, for the first time, I looked in a sort of mirror and saw other badly burned children. The reflection unnerved me.

I had gone through the first two months thinking this awful thing that happened only happened to me, and somehow, rather than feeling victimized, I felt happy to have survived. I felt special, and not necessarily in a bad way. But in the three long weeks that followed in a Boston burn ward, I came to the horrible realization that I was a member of some rather sick and horrid club. Where did all these other children come from? Why were they here? Why did this happen to so many children?

Although I was medically stable at the time, I was placed in the intensive ward at the Shriners due to overcrowding on the convalescent wing. To my left was a little girl in a plastic tent, Sandy, a two-year-old with burns over her entire body. To my right was Joey, a nine-year-old with extensive and disfiguring burns who cried and whimpered through the days and nights. The rest of the ward was filled to capacity. Fifteen severely burned children in one small open ward. My father would later recall the first time he entered the ward. He said it was the closest thing to hell he had ever seen.

My parents had jobs and three other children back in Connecticut, so during the week, I was alone with my new fellow patients. School had started, and my mom dutifully brought handouts from my new fifth-grade teacher for me to complete. I ignored them. My hometown of Canton, and school, seemed so far away. I came from a small town, but the burn ward was an even smaller town.

My best friend on the ward was another ten-year-old boy from Malden, Massachusetts named Jody Nolan. Jody had been burned in a terrible camping accident that took the lives of his only sister, two brothers, his father, and his dog. His mother and an older brother who were shopping at the time were spared. Jody would sit with me, and he would show me a picture of his sister that he always carried with him. "She's beautiful, isn't she?" he'd say. "My sister was beautiful." He described for me, in a calm and matter-of-fact way, how he watched his family members drop dead one by one as he himself burned.

We sat on the edge of my bed under the white fluorescent lights. I was quiet.

I liked Jody a lot, and he liked me.

He was a sweet and kind boy with a wonderful, loving mother. Once, when I experienced severe abdominal pain likely due to narcotic induced constipation, Jody sat with me on my bed and rubbed my belly until the pain went away.

The east wing of the Shriner's was a windowless, dark, open ward with a central nursing station surrounded on three walls by fifteen beds, half of them open, the rest encased in clear plastic tents with constantly humming air-circulating blowers. It was always chaotic. It was never quiet. Someone was always moaning or crying out in pain.

Among us children, there was whispered talk of death, like other children might talk of someone going to the principal's office. Children who had been on the ward or those who never survived out of the ER. But the adults never talked to us about such things, so we were left to contemplate them by ourselves, especially at night when the ward grew relatively quiet and most of the adults had gone home.

At times, owing to the harsh reality of our circumstances, we were not even treated like children. Once, an overwhelmed night shift nurse approached me asking for help.

"Could you read this book to Rodney, the little boy in tent one by the door? I just did his dressing change, and I gave him a pain shot. He'll be asleep soon, but I have to do a dressing change on Joey. I'm sure Rodney would really like it if you'd read him a story."

Happy to be of help, I shuffled over to the chair at the side of his clear plastic tent. As Rodney moaned softly, I read the storybook until he was asleep. When he had nodded off, I gazed upon his naked, burnt body. Burns covered eighty-five percent of it. He did not rest on a bed. He was suspended by orthopedic wires hooked to long pins that passed through his skin and through the center of his long bones so that his denuded tissue would not rest on the sheets.

"Goodnight, Rodney," I said, and returned to my own bed next to Sandy, the two-year-old burned baby.

I drifted through my hospital days by dealing with one thing at a time, dealing with only those things that I absolutely had to deal with. I was grateful for the moments when the Demerol numbed both my body and my mind. In between pain shots, the only thing I knew how to do was power through the immediate challenge—the dressing change, the skin grafts, the physical therapy, the wound debridement, almost always something painful—by trying to be a good soldier. Trying to get through it all.

There was no space for reflection on what was happening. I focused all my energy and effort on simply surviving—one minute at a time.

COMING HOME

And then one day, they sent me home. It seemed so abrupt. Discharged so suddenly from the burn ward. I returned to my home in the woods of my sleepy little town.

My parents were relieved to have me home. The three-hour commutes to Boston and the extra attention and care I had required while I was in the hospital had exhausted them. They made it clear to me, to my great disappointment, that my special status as the medically fragile child who soaked up disproportionate parental time and effort was expiring. It was time to get back to normal. It horrified me to learn that I would be unpacking all my boxes of gifts and cards from the hospital by myself! I would never suffer from a lack of attention or affection from either of my parents, but it was time to get back to normal.

My brother, Bruce, accepted my return to the home with little comment. We never spoke of the accident or what had happened, but then he wasn't one to talk about much of anything, so I thought little of it. And yet, despite his aloofness and taciturn nature, we remained close, just in a mostly nonverbal way. Still, while we continued to do things together, like building forts or riding bikes, we were different people, and we were drifting apart.

I had a love for him that was special. We had both survived that gas can explosion. We shared that. Our job now, it seemed, was to move on. One foot in front of the other. On two completely different paths.

My two younger sisters seemed happy to have me home but were a little nervous around me when I first returned. Even at six and three, they understood I had changed and not just physically. They were tentative in their interactions, as if I was a new person in the home. Their apparent discomfort with me made me feel a little sad. It was as if I had become something scary or even inhuman. But in time, they grew accustomed to the new normal, and they became more at ease around me. I was settling back into my home, but things had clearly changed.

John, the friend who was with us when the gas can exploded, had been visiting from the Netherlands with his family when the accident occurred. He and his family had already returned to Europe, and I would not see him again for many years.

I reentered the school in fifth grade. Having survived the burn ward, it seems, was the easy part. My reentry into the "normal" world was a bitch. The world I had once known—the cold leafy bus stops of the rural New England autumn, the long bouncy bus rides to the aging brick institutional public middle school, all my old friends—all were dissociated from the cruel but hidden world I had experienced.

The first thing my buddy Eric asked me when I returned to my fifth-grade classroom from the burn hospital was, "Did the nurses see you naked?"

He and my other friends snickered as they gathered around my desk, giddy with the thought of me being naked in front of a grown woman. In that moment, I knew my peers could not understand what I had survived. I turned and walked away from Eric. I did not respond to his taunt or the laughter of my friends.

These guys are assholes, I thought to myself. They have no fucking idea.

My best friend, Tim, came after me. "Just forget about them. They don't know anything," he said. Tim was quiet and easygoing by nature. I realized I needed his friendship and loyalty more than I needed words. Tim was a little like Jody at Shriners. A good guy who would help me get through those difficult early days back at school just by being present and quietly accepting of who I had become.

In the coming days and years, I did my level best to reinsert myself to the superficial suspended reality of everyday life. Back to the schoolbooks that failed to hold my interest. Back to being a class clown. I went back to as close to a normal life as I could muster. I did a pretty good job. On good days, which were most, I even fooled myself. Life seemed okay. Being burned was awful, but the worst was behind me now.

I was plucky and determined, and hell, I already knew I was a survivor. My burns had disfigured a third of my body, and I had very visible red keloid scars on the right side of my face, right arm, back, right leg, and inner left leg. My right hand got the worst of it. The fire had destroyed the outer two joints of the four fingers of my right hand. The injured fingers had healed across the destroyed joint space, bone to bone, so my hand was frozen into a misshaped claw. With the awkwardly fused joints, I had been told by my music teacher to abandon the flute, which was fine with me. I don't know what I was thinking when I chose that instrument. I switched to trombone, which was much cooler, and served as therapy in working out my flexion contractures in my right elbow.

"He'll regain some functional use out of that right hand—but he probably won't play the piano again," Dr. Dutton had informed my parents. My playing, prior to the injury, had been little to crow about, so this loss would not have been mourned by the music world. I hadn't really even enjoyed it as beginning music students so often don't. But that comment sure got under my skin. Screw him, I thought. I'm going to play the piano. I snuck into the piano room when no one was around, and, over a matter of weeks, slowly worked up a little piece from last year's recital. Then, when I was ready, I sat down and played it when I knew my mom was within hearing range.

"You're playing the piano!" she said, surprised and very pleased.

You bet your ass I am. No high-on-his-horse doctor is gonna tell me what I can or can't do. What the hell does he know about me, anyway?

So, in this way, I largely put the burns in my past and moved forward. There would be further short admissions to the hospital for scar revisions, and physical therapy would continue for a few more years. But I was focused on new things. I would master the piano. I could conquer any adversity. Put any barrier in my way, and I would find a way to push through it.

Still, while I lived the essentially happy life of a smart-aleck clown, I always knew that there was more to this place than my mundane surroundings revealed in a typical suburban fifth grader's world. And if anything crept across my path that related to that other world I knew, I would seize on it. Though ignorant about most current affairs, I was aware at the age of ten that the United States was at war in Vietnam. Dr. Dutton had just returned from treating burn patients there, which was why he felt comfortable treating me in my local hospital. Through him, I felt a connection to that war.

I was not a reader, but I looked at the comics and the pictures in the newspaper. Once, when I was about six, my dad caught my brother and I looking at one of his *Playboy* magazines. My brother tried to defend himself.

"I just look at the comics."

"Yes," I added. "And I just look at the pictures!"

Yes, I just looked at the pictures. I was not a reader. All I saw in newspapers and magazines were pictures and the comics. In my first months back from the hospital, I was looking at the pictures in a news magazine when I saw something that stopped me cold. It was like it was a special postcard to me from the other side, from the world beyond the Shriners Hospital. The picture was of Kim Phuc, a nine-year-old Vietnamese girl who was burned in a napalm explosion in Vietnam just two months before my own accident.

In the picture, Kim Phuc was running down the road towards the camera. Naked. Her clothes were burned off her body. Shock and horror on her face. I understood that she was real. I knew it. I felt it. I could explain it to no one, and despite being surrounded by love and nurturing, from my family, from my friends, and from my school, I was totally alone in seeing what I saw in the way that I saw it. There it was. It was real.

Wouldn't my friends just laugh at her nakedness?

I thought about Kim Phuc often and was deeply moved by the thought of her pain and suffering. She was like Jody Nolan. She was like Sandy. Kim Phuc was like me.

On returning to the fifth grade at Canton Middle School, I came upon a copy of a 1951 book in the library called *We of Nagasaki,* written by Dr. Takashi Nagai. The librarian immediately came over to me as I picked up the book. Naturally, all the teachers and staff at my school knew I had just returned from a burn hospital, and she must have been mindful that the book might upset me. She calmly explained that the book was an account by survivors of an atomic bomb blast. I was intrigued. I insisted on signing it out.

An atomic bomb? What the hell was an atomic bomb?

I was a lousy reader at ten. We had a chart on the board in our classroom and our teacher, Mrs. Patchen, placed a sticker next to our name for every book we read outside of school. By the end of the school year, most kids had ten or twelve stickers. Martha Porter had thirty-seven. I had three.

One of those three books was *We of Nagasaki.* I read the whole damn thing. It blew my mind. I could not put it down. I would not forget it. Ever. I knew it was real. I had been to that place. It existed. In an important way, reading this book was an affirmation of what I knew to be true.

In school, we watched a film that, likely for lack of resources, they showed year after year. The film was based on the book *Flatland* by Edwin Abbott, and it told the story of a triangle from the two-dimensional world who gets blown off the two-dimensional grid into the third dimension. And of course, his entire perspective changes. And when he returns to the second dimension, he tries to explain what he now understands about reality to the residents of the two-dimensional world. And he fails. I identified with that poor triangle. Here's what I now knew and could not unknow: We live, and we die. We suffer. Pain can be overwhelming and while it can be ameliorated, it cannot be vanquished. Whether or not you want to accept those truths, they are true. And with that perspective, I no longer viewed my life or the lives of others with a consciousness based merely in the present.

I was like the needle on a long-playing record: I experienced life where my needle rode the groove in forward marching time, but at any given point, I was aware of the entire record, from beginning to end. I knew the music wouldn't always be pleasing. I knew that some records were long, while others were unmercifully short. Yes, I knew that the record definitely ends.

I was also beginning to understand this truth: very bad things happen to people, even little children. In my case, it was an accident, and, if anyone was to blame, it was me. Now I was realizing that sometimes people intentionally did these things to children. The more I looked around, the more evidence I saw of suffering. I learned that before Vietnam there had been the Korean War. That was the war depicted on *M*A*S*H*, the new show that I watched and loved from my hospital bed. It was at that time, inspired by Dr. Dutton and the character of Hawkeye Pierce, that I decided I would be a doctor when I grew up.

Still, even with the war grinding on in Vietnam, there was no war anywhere near my home. In Canton, we lived in peace. But I felt connected to the suffering of other people I was learning about, even those who came before me or those who lived very far away. In 1973, when the first American prisoners of war were released, Winsted, Connecticut, welcomed the local hero James Walsh home from his captivity in Vietnam. I read about him in the paper with intense interest. Captain Walsh had evaded death when his plane was shot down. I sensed he knew what I knew.

After the Nagasaki book, I read *Slaughterhouse-Five* by Kurt Vonnegut. I was definitely not the reader in my family, but my brother Bruce, only eleven, was already reading adult novels. My parents placed no restrictions on what he read. Normally, I wasn't interested in what Bruce read, but he seduced me by showing me Vonnegut's simple line drawing of a starlet's boobs in between the book's printed words. Then, he pointed out naughty limericks. Okay. This book might be worth a try.

And I learned that Billy Pilgrim had become unstuck in time. Billy survived the firebombing of Dresden, and after that, he never just saw the present. He saw the entire record album, from beginning to end, too. Only his needle jumped around on the record. But I got it. I loved Billy Pilgrim. I loved Kurt Vonnegut and his surviving Dresden. I loved him for what he knew and could not unknow. And I love how he just dealt with it. With melancholy and dark humor. It gave me hope.

And through all of this, I never stopped thinking about Sandy, the little two-year-old girl in the tent next to me. Jody told me that Sandy was not in the hospital because of an accident. She was there because someone did something to her.

This was the truth that was revealed to me as a boy: the world is brutally cruel and unforgiving. No one in my world back at home seemed to understand this. It was my secret to carry.

But I also understood I was not totally alone in knowing this secret. My buddies from the Shriners, certainly Jody Nolan, knew. At the Shriners, we all knew. The truth.

Kim Phuc knew. Kurt Vonnegut and Billy Pilgrim knew.

There were people out there somewhere who would understand me.

I wanted to talk to someone, anyone, who knew what I knew. I wanted to share what was inside me and even made timid attempts to share my thoughts with my closest friends.

But no one I knew in my small town seemed to understand.

Not at all.

So, I buried the truth.

MAUREEN AND MUSIC

Very early in my reentry from the hospital, as I was finding my way among my old friends in Mrs. Patchen's fifth-grade class, I noticed the brown-haired girl with beautiful eyes in the fifth-grade classroom across the hall. I noticed her in a way I had never noticed a girl before. The girl had gone to school with me since the second grade. But now, something was different. The way I saw everything had changed. Thinking about her made me feel...*good*.

Her name was Maureen. Her father was the pharmacist, and he was a neighbor and a friend of my grandparents. I rather quickly became obsessed with her. I would grade each day by whether or not I caught a mere glimpse of her returning in the single file line from the cafeteria or maybe waiting for her bus. Naturally, even though it would have been technically possible to approach her during free periods such as recess or in the cafeteria, fifth-grade decorum strictly forbid such brazen and reckless behavior. Anyway, my face was scarred, and I wore a series of awkward custom braces on my right arm to correct for flexion contractures resulting from the burns. I was not in peak courting condition.

So, I took an indirect approach.

I began this indirect approach through my friendship with Jeff.

Jeff was a classmate of Maureen's. Jeff and I had a bit of a foundation in that we were both recognized as the class artists, an association established years earlier when I sketched an Easter Bunny holding an electric guitar on my first day of school as a new student in the second grade. "Cool!" my classmates said. "That's even better than Jeff Rannenberg can draw." Jeff was quickly summoned. He looked over the bunny with a critical eye. "Yes," he graciously conceded. "It is better than anything I can do."

So, for much of my fifth-grade year, I would seize any opportunity—before the morning bell rang, returning from gym class, in line for the cafeteria—to drift out of Mrs. Patchen's door into the hallway for a little spontaneous rendezvous with Jeff, who would always be looking for me too. I genuinely liked Jeff, and we quickly found we had the same silly sense of humor. The point—or at least so Jeff must have thought—of these little encounters was for one of us to say something silly and see how cleverly the other responded. This indeed was great fun, but the real point for me was to peek over his shoulder into THE room for a glimpse…just a glimpse…and dare I even think it, if Jeff and I were funny enough, maybe a small crowd would gather (it did happen), and maybe she would notice (she didn't).

But it was mostly a dream. It was mostly all in my head. I kept thinking of her. I kept thinking of her because…because thinking of her stopped an inner nonphysical noise that was always buzzing in my head. The psychic noise was ever present—a dissonant emotional hum that had kept me on edge ever since the gasoline explosion. It was a haunting din arising from the fact that the pieces of my world in the hospital did not fit together with the pieces of my life back home. It was an internal noise that made me feel like I no longer belonged in this world. That, perhaps, I could not continue in this world. I was not suicidal, but I was desperate to find some way to make the dissonant noise stop.

The thought of her was escapism, but it was much more than that. It really was a powerful analgesia. And more than just analgesia, it was my first small step towards reconnecting with something like a normal life. Or as close to normal as I could get. It would never be normal.

I suppose, then, what kept me going was an obsession to find that there was something more to this life than what I had experienced. Something good. Something warm. Something with meaning. Something comforting. Something that would make the pain stop even for a moment. Something that would serve as an antidote to the overwhelming darkness I could not unsee.

I believe I rather easily could have used drugs in the years that followed. I already knew and loved the narcotics they had treated me with in the hospital. They made the noise go away—for a little while. But I was scared of them. I knew I would have no control over them. I had begged Dr. Dutton, my burn surgeon, not to taper me off them even when I no longer needed them for physical pain. I so craved Demerol that not only would I have robbed for it; I believe I would have killed for it. I asked Dr. Dutton why he was taking away my pain medication. He explained that I had become dependent, and needed increasing doses to feel better, and at some point, at higher doses, the medicine would stop my breathing. I would die. And for that reason, once weaned off the drugs, I was ever mindful of their power to destroy me. They were not the solution to my problem.

But just maybe, Maureen was.

I remember one day after school waiting in the auditorium for my bus to be called. Maureen's bus group sat directly in front of mine, so this was the highlight of my day. I knew I would see her. Well, I knew I would see the back of her head. And then one day, she sat down in the seat directly in front of me. I had never been so close. It is difficult to describe the wonder I experienced staring self-consciously at every strand of straight and glorious brown hair on the back of that perfectly shaped head. So close I could have touched it.

Once, when I was seeing Dr. Dutton in follow-up, he asked me why I wasn't doing my exercises for my limb contractures. "Why should I?" I challenged him. "I don't care if I can't fully extend my arm or legs." I really didn't. I was, and am, quite lazy about physical exertion. And I hated sports because I was awful at all of them.

"Well, someday you will care," he replied. "Someday you will want to chase girls, and when that day comes, I want you to be able to catch them."

I thought of Maureen, and thereafter, I did my exercises without protest.

In the sixth grade, my obsession grew. It took on a new dimension. The main social change from fifth grade to sixth, as I recall, is that boys and girls began to interact just a little bit more. I had the great—and I do mean great—fortune of having an assigned seat in Mr. Larco's class situated behind Cindy and in front of Linda. Cindy, Linda, and I became good friends over that year (it was Cindy who happily shared details about the menstruation lecture that Dr. Diters gave the girls when me and all the other boys were sent to the gym to occupy ourselves with a few raggedy basketballs). Cindy was my first confidant of the opposite sex, a wonderful relationship that would continue for the rest of my school years. Both Cindy and Linda were genuinely sweet and, as a bonus, lovely to look at.

While I basked in the glory and symmetry that was Cindy and Linda, the thrilling thing was that Linda was both a neighbor and close friend of Maureen. So, one day I shared my secret. I told Cindy first, because I always felt more natural and at ease around Cindy. I told her I really liked Maureen Grinvalsky.

"Really," Cindy replied. "Did you tell her?"

Did I *what*? Cindy just laughed.

When Linda learned, she just smiled. "That's so nice. You should tell her."

Right.

Whether Linda ever told her, I still don't know. But I sure didn't. I never said a word to her.

In seventh grade, we entered junior high school. Maureen was still the girl of my dreams, and I can't even begin to count up the endless hours consumed by daydreaming about things like, you know, maybe someday we'll actually talk, or maybe I might make a joke and she will laugh (a big score by my thinking), or maybe…maybe our eyes might accidentally meet?

ACROSS A BRIDGE OF FIRE

This is how I coped.

Then something happened.

My grandmother told me that Maureen and her mother and sister had been involved in a terrible car accident. They were badly injured and were in the hospital. A child in the other car had been killed.

In a flash, my little house of comfort cards came crashing down.

I was devastated. I was frozen and for a moment, everything stopped. But only for a moment. And then in a weird way, it all made sense.

I understand this. I get this. And I know how to handle this!

I set to work almost immediately, drawing pictures for Maureen. I holed up in my room at home to the soundtrack of *Something New* by the Beatles and drew pictures. You see, as the well-established class artist (in a very small school) this was the greatest gift I could bestow. I struggled to produce my greatest works, a series of pictures that included a picture of Maureen's father standing behind the counter of his pharmacy, and others of knights on horseback and who knows what else. I was an artist consumed with his muse. This would be how I would break through. I would let her know I existed. I would make the connection.

When I was done with the portfolio, my grandmother delivered the pictures and a get-well card to the Grinvalsky home where Maureen and her mother and sister were expected to return any day from the hospital.

And then it happened. Mrs. Grinvalsky called my house and spoke to my mother. My mother turned to me and said, "Mrs. Grinvalsky thought you might like to come to dinner tomorrow. Maureen is coming home from the hospital."

Me? Dinner? The Grinvalskys'? She might as well have just said I had been invited to dinner in heaven.

Twelve years old. I had never been invited to a girl's house. And now it had happened, and it was not just any girl. It was THE girl. And she has just been in a hospital after a terrible accident. I didn't know any other kids at my school that had been in accidents. I was happy. I was so hopeful.

The day came. I was deposited on the front step of the house. A door opened. The rest is almost entirely a blur. I remember Maureen, sitting on the couch in her living room, unable to move easily due to her hip fracture and other injuries. I remember her smile. I remember her being so natural and at ease. I was neither. I remember her mother. As a kid, I always found it easier to relate to the parents. Maureen's mother saved me by helping with conversation whenever it lagged because she was a natural talker. Maureen and I swapped a few stories about life in the hospital. We talked about our scars. She thanked me for the pictures. I must have blathered on about the Beatles and she confided that she loved to listen to music too. Like me, she took piano lessons and remembered how I had played "The Entertainer" in front of everyone at school. We had melon before dinner—apparently her family often did this. It was so foreign and refined to me.

The time passed much too quickly. The visit came to an end, and I said my thank-yous and goodbyes.

The thought of Maureen was so warm and comforting. Although highly anxious in her presence, from a safe distance, the thought of her calmed and comforted me, much like the narcotics, and later, the music of the Beatles did.

Before being burned, I always liked music. But the year before I was burned, I discovered the Beatles *White Album*, and I entered a new and wonderful world.

For me, the hum, the existential ringing in my ears of the dark secrets of the world gave me no rest. But one of the few things other than the thought of Maureen that would make the dissonant hum settle down was music. Beatles music. I listened to it endlessly on a small suitcase record player in my room or on an old stereo in our basement. I learned to play Beatles songs on the piano. And with the sixty-seven dollars I had collected from gifts from family and friends while I was hospitalized, I bought a Yamaha acoustic guitar from Clavier Music and my neighbor Sandy McMullin taught me a few chords. With the joints in my right hand permanently frozen, I had to learn to play right-handed even though I am left-handed, but having learned that way, I never thought much about it.

Music made all the bad stuff go away. Without it, I think, I would have died. And when I listened to it, I entered another world. It was intense. It was three dimensional. And like any other addiction, I had to do it every day. Listen to it. Play it on my piano or guitar. Like I needed it to breathe.

I had the hopeful idea that maybe Maureen felt the same way.

And that is how I made it through those early days—by listening to the Beatles and thinking endlessly about a girl.

THE STRIP CLUB FIRE

The smoke appeared to be rising from the strip club. Even though we were too young to have ever been inside, we all knew exactly where it was, and we had a pretty good idea what went on inside.

It was six years after coming home from the hospital after my accident, and we were sixteen-year-old boys who had just survived our junior year of high school and had a car.

We probably should have resisted the pull of curiosity that drew us towards the fire like moths to a porch light. But judgment is not the forte of teenage boys. In fact, summer had just begun. We had our restless souls, but nothing even remotely resembling a plan.

"It's Male Dominick's," Press declared. "The strip club is on fire."

"Let's check it out," Chris suggested.

The possibilities of a strip club fire on a hot Memorial Day were powerfully seductive; still, at least I should have known better. I really should have. But I said nothing. Press swerved his Fiat convertible off Route 44 into the parking lot of the business behind the club.

The three of us climbed up out of the convertible, our eyes transfixed on the long, grey, ordinary single-story building that we had never been permitted to enter. Thick, black smoke poured out of the rear. Red flames danced from a single broken window and snaked up towards the roof.

"Let's cut through here," Chris, the analytical one, said. He pointed to a cluster of trees behind the club. "We'll never get close in front, and the fire is definitely coming from the back of the building. C'mon, guys."

"Male Dominick's" was as out of place as a small-town business could be—a strip club in Canton, a quiet bedroom community twenty minutes northwest of Hartford. Yet the irascible and libertarian Mr. Dominick had thwarted every effort by local officials to close his enterprise. While there were many in town who wished he and his tawdry business would disappear, he provided a service, and he had his customers, and as he was all too ready to remind the town selectman, he had his rights.

The annual Memorial Day parade marking the beginning of our summer had just ended a half hour earlier. Chris and I had marched as members of the Canton High School band, and Press, who was a little too laid-back and cool to be in the band, had come down to the parade to heckle us.

Canton was a small town, and the band was a concert band, not a marching band, as our new band director, Mr. Gaedeke, had tried in vain to argue before the parade organizers. But the members of the VFW were not going to march without a marching band. So, there we were, in our ill-fitting maroon band uniforms, a slide trombone to my lips and a trumpet to Chris's, bleating out a serviceable rendition of John Phillip Sousa's "South Rampart Street Parade." We struggled to not lose our pitch when we broke into grins each time the drummers screwed up the cadence and the veterans lost their marching step.

None of us could forget how the leader of the local VFW had berated Mr. Gaedeke at the end of last year's arrhythmic fiasco. "My veterans need a solid cadence to march to!" the veteran in the faded green uniform two sizes too small shouted at poor Mr. Gaedeke, who was conspicuously dressed in civilian clothes. "You call yourself a bandleader? My goddamn granddaughter can pound out a more regular beat than your lousy drummers can! These men risked their lives so that you could go study art and music at some fancy college.

The least you can do is show them some respect by laying down a decent beat that they can march to!"

It wasn't much of a parade, and if the voluntary fire departments of Canton and Collinsville had not marched in their dress blues behind the oldest and newest bright red fire engines, it would have been a very short parade indeed. But the volunteer fire department was a sizeable and enthusiastic crew, and their dress blues saw about as much action as our polyester band uniforms. When the parade was over, we ditched our silly uniforms and jumped in Press's Fiat and went looking for trouble, girls, and ideally both.

We had arrived at the club fire ahead of the first trucks, and it occurred to me that the parade, which had passed directly in front of the Collinsville Fire Station, probably disrupted the process of deploying a crew to respond to the fire. But the club was no more than a mile away from the station, and within several minutes, four trucks came roaring towards the smoking strip club, with their lights flashing and sirens blaring. As they pulled up to the front of the building, the first firefighters in firefighting gear jumped down and set about unraveling hoses to fight the blaze. We watched events unfold from our unique position in the parking lot behind the burning club. One of the firefighters ran to the back of the building near where we stood and started kicking at the back door. After a few kicks, the door gave, immediately releasing an explosive burst of thick smoke. The fireman paused just long enough to let most of the smoke clear from the doorway before he darted into the burning building. We collectively held our breaths. Seconds later, he bolted back out into the parking lot, bent over, hands clutching his knees as he coughed and gasped for air.

In no time, a crowd was gathering out front. The strip club was along the main two-lane highway that cut through town, and half the people leaving the parade would have to pass by it on their way home. In a matter of minutes, the crowd grew to about a hundred. More than half were firefighters who had congregated at the firehouse following the parade. Most of them were still in their dress blue uniforms. Almost all of them lingered among the civilian onlookers as they watched the strip club spit smoke and fire.

Just then, the car of the fire chief pulled up to the building, and Chief Drs (he had a vowel-free surname that rhymes with furs) jumped out and ran towards the fire. He slowed up as he approached the first truck and shouted something to the firefighters, who were setting up hoses. He pointed towards the hydrants and then towards the flames now advancing on the roof. Then he jogged towards the back of the building where my friends and I stood. He was met there by the same firefighter who had attempted to enter the structure moments earlier.

"I tried to get inside, Chief, but the smoke is too thick!" the fireman shouted.

"Is there anyone inside?" Chief Drs asked, pointing towards the back door.

"I don't know. But the owner called in the alarm, and we haven't been able to account for him."

"Well then, dammit, why the hell is everyone just standing around? Let's get in that building! Come on! Get someone up on that roof. Now! Let's go!"

I knew Chief Drs as Mr. Ken Drs, and I looked up to him. He was a tough guy and a straight talker who stood tall. I was at an age when I needed role models.

Smoke continued to gush through the broken window. Within minutes, a lone figure appeared on the roof.

"Oh, my god," I gasped. "That's Mr. Drs up there!" I pointed to the roof of the burning club where Ken Drs was with an axe, chopping a ventilation hole in the roof. Mr. Drs was the father of our classmate, Kari. We knew he was recovering from a heart attack only a few months earlier. "What's he doing?"

"Wow. He better be careful," was all Chris could say. Press was silent. We all looked on in amazement. No sooner was the thick smoke venting through the newly created roof opening than Mr. Drs was scrambling down off the roof and entering the building, immediately followed by three fellow firefighters. Moments later, he and his colleagues reemerged in a haze of smoke, hacking and coughing and carrying the blackened and nearly limp body of the old man. Mr.

Dominick. The smoke cleared. There, a few yards away from our prime perch behind the club, the purveyor of flesh lay heaving and gasping. His own skin, freshly licked by flames, was blackened and peeling.

The only other time in my short life I had smelled burnt human hair was six years earlier when it was my own. The only other time I had smelled burning flesh, it was my own.

I shouldn't have been there.

Mr. Dominick choked weakly as the firemen laid him down in front of us on the pavement. Someone called out for the ambulance crew.

The smell of burned flesh entered my lungs and momentarily cut off my breath. I felt woozy. I steadied myself and looked at Mr. Drs as he went about directing his men. They lifted Mr. Dominick to a stretcher. I watched Mr. Drs, and I took a deep breath. I felt numb and weak.

Mr. Drs stood there like a fucking rock.

I gathered all the strength I could muster. I was outside my body. Above and to the left.

Finally, Press spoke. "Let's get out of here."

"Yeah. All right. I've seen enough," Chris replied.

Somehow, I managed to walk back to the car and climb into the cramped back seat.

We were later to learn that Mr. Dominick survived to the hospital, but he died that night from his burns.

THE MOVIE AND
THE PHOTOGRAPH

They say there is nothing so powerful as a smell to trigger memory. For me, there is no more powerful smell than the smell of burnt flesh and hair. The strip club fire had rattled me. It disturbed all those things I had tried to bury so deep down inside. That's when my buddy Jeff and I went to see the new movie *The Deer Hunter*.

The movie depicted the brutal journey of three men from Pennsylvania through their traumas in Vietnam. The Russian roulette scenes were getting a lot of attention in the press. But it was the very brief inclusion of actual news footage from the fall of South Vietnam just four years earlier that grabbed me. The scenes of refugees fleeing the advancing Vietnamese communists and the utter chaos of war quickened my pulse. I felt some sort of connection to these people. After seeing the movie, I could not get the thought of the Vietnamese refugees out of my mind.

I don't know what the original connection to the Vietnam thing was. Could it have been the profoundly affecting photo of nine-year-old Kim Phuc running burned and naked from the napalm flames that had become one of the most symbolic photographs of the war? Could it have been that, as boys, my buddy Scott Clark and I had eagerly gathered up and proudly wore the cast aside helmets and fatigues of Scott's neighbor Fritz Feibel, a recently returned soldier who happily gave us his military equipment on returning from Vietnam? That Dr. Dutton had just returned from Vietnam? Or was it simply that the television war of my youth was among the rare evidence to me that I was not completely crazy?

The Deer Hunter was the first war movie I can recall seeing where the characters were fully developed as ordinary and relatable men before we see them crashed into a stunning explosion of brutality in battle, an approach that made their transition from the slow-paced world of the Pennsylvania steel mills and Allegheny Mountains to the violence and chaos of Vietnam both soul crushing and poignant. That abrupt transition from the post-hunting alcohol-soaked bar to a village with burned and bloody bodies hit me deep in the pit of my stomach. Yes, I thought. I know this.

When the young steelworkers-turned-soldiers return from Vietnam, no one really understands them, and in a way, no one really wants to know what they had been through. This reverberated within me like a clanging bell. When I returned from the hospital, my school peers did not understand what I was dealing with. As I came to realize that they didn't even have the vocabulary or experience to draw upon, I just accepted that, like *Alice in Wonderland*, I had been through the looking glass into a world I would never be able to explain. The men on the screen were playing out that story, too. They were playing the role I was already living.

In one scene, Robert De Niro's character Michael drives by his own welcome home party to seek solitude in a hotel room. Alone, he collapses to the floor. Even at sixteen, I completely understood the scene. When Christopher Walken's Nick was rendered mute when a military doctor tried to engage with him in a Saigon hospital, I saw myself.

My peers seemed unperturbed by the struggles of the world—a blessing of youth and innocence. On very rare occasions, I made efforts to talk to my friends about how I saw things. There was the day I came across a picture in a school library copy of *LIFE* magazine. The picture, taken by photographer Susan Meiselas, was captioned "Maimed Children of Civil War in Nicaragua." The photograph was taken moments after Somoza's planes had bombed the district in an assault on Sandinista guerillas. They had brought the children wounded into a church in their barrio. I could see the shock and disbelief on the faces of the children. I knew that feeling. Pain. Numbness. These children had fallen off the edge of the earth. I could not look at this picture without feeling compelled to do something, although at the time, I knew not what that would be.

It did not matter that it was Nicaragua. It could have been anywhere. But I knew I lived in a world where that kind of suffering—especially for children—appeared to be far away. And while I was happy that it was far away, it was still real.

I showed the picture of the injured Nicaraguan children to a few friends. "What's that? That's gross. Why are you looking at that? Hey, what are you doing after study hall?"

I didn't even try to push it. I knew there was no point. I was frustrated by my friends, but I knew nothing was wrong with them. Something was wrong with me.

Prior to being burned, I was an uneven student, easily distractible and mildly disruptive to my class because of my constant need to make people laugh. I had suffered under a series of terrible teachers, including Mrs. Gleszer who had visited me in the hospital. When I came home from the hospital, my parents, who were teachers themselves, did not leave my classroom assignment to chance after everything I had just gone through. They made sure I had the best teachers going forward. With kinder teachers and a little extra care and attention, I began to thrive academically. In the next few years, I moved from remedial math and reading to the age-appropriate group, and by high school, I was moved to the advanced curriculum. In the meantime, my musical and artistic talents blossomed. Through humor, I became popular, and my peers seemed to think I was smart.

Something in me had changed, but I couldn't say what it was. Somehow, I became more focused and engaged. When teachers told me I had done well on something, it surprised me because I wasn't aware that I had done anything differently. I was still making jokes at the wrong times, but teachers were starting to tell my parents that I was smart. Eventually, the school independent study coordinator, Rosa Matesky, had me tested for my IQ. No one was more surprised than me when she explained I had tested into the special educational category for "gifted students."

I was also beginning to chafe at the constrained structure of a small-town high school. I was eager to get back out into that bigger world that I knew was out there. As a so-called "gifted student," I was allowed to develop an individualized curriculum for myself in my senior year with only two scheduled classes, the rest being independent study. I secured a job, thirty hours a week during school hours, at the Mintz and Hoke Advertising Agency. While I was pretty determined to go into medicine, my other passions were art and music, and advertising seemed to be a potential career path. It was an exciting opportunity, and the founders of the agency encouraged my interest, allowing me to move about freely and join in on most meetings, including creative brainstorming sessions. I loved being at Mintz and Hoke and it kept me distracted for a little while.

Mrs. Matesky supervised my work-study program. She was a kind and nurturing woman. She, as much as anybody, sensed the restlessness in me. Like others, she struggled to understand me. Then, one day, she had a moment of insight.

"I know what your problem is," she said to me one morning. "I know exactly what your problem is. You're searching for truth. Aren't you?"

In *The Deer Hunter*, De Niro articulates a simple philosophy that he summarizes with the phrase "one shot."

"A deer should be taken with one shot. One shot is what it is all about. You try to tell people. They won't listen."

One shot.

You try to tell people. They won't listen.

I was struggling internally with unresolved feelings and festering emotional wounds stemming from the accident and the bigger world, as I had come to understand it. The darker world, where people were killed or injured, where wars were fought, where bombs were dropped, where children were burned. That world had no clear connection to my high school life unfolding in the setting of the morally ambiguous, pot-filled haze of late seventies in suburban, white, middle-class America—but had everything to do with what I had seen on the burn ward.

Despite the intrusive memories from my past, and my intense awareness of horrific events occurring in the wider world, I was not morose or withdrawn. In contrast, I was an overachieving class clown, more known for my sense of humor than for my deep thoughts. I was a class president. I never lost an election from sixth grade until I resigned as a high school junior, a move that possibly marked the earliest anticipation of my eventual departure. Yet I was just as likely to be held for detention after school for all too frequent irreverent behavior towards my teachers in the eternal pursuit of a laugh from my peers. I virtually shut down the school in a spontaneous absurd memorial ceremony for a carrot, causing great distress to my social studies teacher when both the principal and school superintendent showed up in his classroom for the event.

I was an artist and a musician who played keyboards and guitar in several fleeting local rock bands at a time when we worshipped the southern rock of Lynyrd Skynyrd, the Allman Brothers Band, and Marshall Tucker, when we sat in smoke-filled basements listening to Led Zeppelin, Jimi Hendrix, J. Geils and the Doors, and of course, the Beatles. Music was my drug. It helped me cope. The piano that I first returned to as a statement of stubborn determination became an instrument of comfort, and I spent so many hours playing that I actually got sort of good and even began composing my own music. I even performed an original piano composition at a high school band concert. I spent hours and hours listening to Beatles records on my tiny record player; the musical landscape they created would become a lifelong refuge for me.

All the while, I continued to fall in love with a series of out-of-reach girls. While Maureen, my post-hospital crush, had become a good friend, and I would spend many more afternoons at her home, I never did ask her out. In time, I went on to fall for other unwinnable girls—Jean, Cindy, Darcy, and Tory—while failing to fully appreciate the beauty and character of the few who showed an interest in me.

As I became even more interested in girls, I became just a little self-conscious about my scars. The scars on the right side of my face, despite having been reduced by surgeries, were prominent: a raised red keloid from my right eye to my jaw and another keloid above my lip. My deformed fingers had been surgically fractured and then pinned and healed into a more functional shape, but my hand was red and still looked like a claw. My back and legs were deeply scarred, even in non-burned areas. The site where my skin grafts had been harvested from my thighs had formed thick scars. But I had come by them by surviving real injuries, and I admit I wore them with bit of pride. I knew I was different, and these scars made that clear to the world. And while I wondered what the girls thought, I can't ever remember any of them ever making me feel uncomfortable because of my acquired deformities.

But in the same way that narcotics worked at first in easing the pain but then only worked with escalating and increasingly dangerous doses as time went on, my once innocent focus on girls devolved into an unhealthy obsession with my best friend Press's older sister Tory. Tory was always kind to me, but she was not the least bit romantically interested in her younger brother's friend, and she stated so clearly to me on numerous occasions. My unwillingness to accept her rejection resulted in a long and unhappy struggle with unrequited affection, and I was disappointed to find myself turning into a jerk in my desperate search for warmth and intimacy.

The idea of a girl was no longer working for me. Music alone was no longer working for me. I needed to find another way out.

I needed to find people who understood me. I need to do something to reach the other people who were suffering. I could not wait.

I had one shot.

You try to tell people. They won't listen.

NEWS FROM THE OTHER SIDE

Not long after seeing *The Deer Hunter*, with my mind still agitated and in turmoil, I left home for an innovative summer residential arts program for creative youth at Wesleyan University. Although this was less than an hour from home, the freedom of minimally supervised college style dormitory living for a sixteen-year-old was liberating.

A young drummer named Leonard befriended me and we spoke the same language of rock music obsession. I had found someone who at least understood that part of me and it was deeply gratifying. Conversations I had with artist mentors and college age counselors continued to broaden my worldview. I was evolving on that elusive search for meaning and purpose. And for some reason those visions of massive destruction in the aftermath of America's involvement in Vietnam remained in my mind. I knew there were more important things going on in the world.

So, that October, when I was back in the small and constraining environment of the small-town high school I had long since outgrown, the first television and newspaper images of starving and sick Cambodian refugees crossing into Thailand grabbed my attention.

I felt the pull immediately. It was *The Deer Hunter*, and it was real. It was happening. Now.

My forward path was becoming clear to me. On the one hand, I could coast through the rest of my senior year, enjoy the usual senior year social rituals, and head off to college…or I could leave the bullshit behind and respond to the real humanitarian crisis in Southeast Asia. I watched the news footage on the network news, frustratingly short snippets from the Cambodian border showing desperate people in a state of starvation.

One shot. You have one shot, not two. That made sense to my seventeen-year-old mind. Cambodians were in crisis now.

I read the morning paper that arrived on our doorstep. On November 1, 1979, the front story headline read "Cambodian Alliance Battles Vietnamese." The story revealed the desperate plight of the Cambodians and described the international appeal for help. Both non-communist and Khmer Rouge forces were engaged in fierce fighting against a common enemy along the mountainous border between Thailand and Cambodia, the Vietnamese forces who had invaded Cambodia and overthrown the Khmer Rouge regime. The fighting had resulted in a flood of refugees coming into Thailand. Tens of thousands were displaced. Refugees were getting caught in the crossfire, getting injured and killed by rockets and artillery. Famine was developing within war-torn Cambodia, and the Vietnamese occupiers were unwilling to open up the border for humanitarian aid to the interior of the country. Said Secretary of State Cyrus Vance, "I can think of no issue now before the world community and before every single nation that can lay a greater claim to our concern and our action."

This was real, and it was happening right now. Everything else in my small-town life seemed superficial and insignificant. Why did no one else see this but me?

As I became consumed with the news out of Southeast Asia, I conceived of a plan to leave school and go to the Cambodian border. The decision was simple and straightforward. I would figure out the logistics. Initially, I shared my plan with only two close friends, Chris and Press.

"Are you sure this is a good idea?" they asked. Though they were skeptical, as longtime friends, they seemed to accept the fact that I was different since returning from the hospital, even if they didn't understand why. They also knew I was stubborn and determined.

I read the high school library copy of the *New York Times* religiously, soaking up every detail from Thailand. The November 12, 1979, *Time* magazine had a cover story entitled "Starvation: Deathwatch in Cambodia." I stared into the pictures of relief workers wondering why I wasn't already there.

The article in *Time* began with this sentence: "It is a country soaked in blood, devastated by war, and its people are starving to death." It described the people. "Stumbling on reed-thin legs through the high elephant grass that grows along the frontier, they form a grisly cavalcade of specters, wrapped in black rags. Many are in the last stages of malnutrition, or are ravaged by such diseases as dysentery, tuberculosis, and malaria. Perhaps the most pathetic images of all are those of tearful, exhausted mothers cradling hollow-eyed children with death's-head faces, their bellies swollen, their limbs as thin and fragile as dried twigs." A congressional delegation including Senator John Danforth had visited the border camps. The senator described the encampments as "ground with people strewn over it." I looked into the vacant eyes of a starving child in a photograph accompanying the article. The eyes of the starving child in the picture looked right at me. They did not move. I could not look away.

The article described the massive international effort to respond, and the political and security barriers that existed. Frustrated by the lack of cooperation of the Vietnamese-backed regime in opening up the ports at Sihanoukville or the airport of Phnom Penh, some had floated the idea of a "land bridge" where aid would be delivered into the interior by truck across the Thai-Cambodian border. It was an unlikely scheme, as the border was the front line of fighting between the Vietnamese invaders, the Khmer Rouge remnants, and the Thai army. It was risky business. The Reverend Theodore Hesburgh of Notre Dame responded to the risk by saying, "I'm perfectly willing to ride in the lead truck and get shot in the process rather than sit back and have it on my conscience that I did nothing to stop a second holocaust."

He was right. I knew that I could not have it on my conscience that I did not act in the face of such suffering.

I had no illusions that I had anything to offer, although I desperately hoped I could be of service, but I knew that I needed to be there. If this was happening right now in the world, I had to be there with those people. I understood that the Cambodian border was somehow connected to the burn ward. That they were part of the same reality that no one else around me seemed to really see or fully comprehend.

These descriptions of what was unfolding in a faraway land came to occupy my mind like an obsession. I thought of little else.

One day in January 1980, while killing time in the high school library, my senior English teacher, Mr. Boldway, approached me. He was holding a copy of the *New York Times Magazine* from the Sunday paper. "You might be interested in this," he said. I've never been sure what provoked this encounter. Had one of my confidants shared my plans with him?

The cover story of the Book Review section was "The Death and Life of Dith Pran" by Sydney Schanberg—the true-life account that would years later be made into the film *The Killing Fields*. It was one of the first widely read accounts of the brutal Khmer Rouge regime, and I read it with deep fascination and horror.

Dith Pran had been an assistant to *New York Times* reporter Sydney Schanberg when he covered the war in Cambodia in the early seventies. When the Khmer Rouge captured Phnom Penh in 1975, Schanberg and other journalists initially tried to stay to cover the new regime, but quickly found themselves holed up in the French embassy, their very lives under threat by a hostile Khmer Rouge. Pran helped negotiate safe passage for Schanberg and the others, but he himself was kicked out of the embassy, and was lost to Schanberg who escaped to the US. Cambodia totally closed itself to the outside world and embarked on a radical effort to return to an agrarian society. Pran was sent to the countryside where he concealed his past and survived as a slave laborer under the Khmer Rouge for the next few years while people around him who were found to have Western sympathies were taken away and executed in the killing fields. Between starvation and executions, thousands of Cambodians perished, and the country was plagued by famine and mass starvation. Pran himself endured starvation and was forced to toil in the fields, always fearful that his past association with Americans would be discovered and he, too, would be executed. But when the Vietnamese invaded Cambodia, Pran seized the opportunity afforded by the chaotic flight of the Khmer Rouge to escape to the Thai border in October 1979, where a malnourished but resilient Dith Pran was reunited with Schanberg.

Reading of Dith Pran's odyssey and struggle to survive made everything in my protected world seem superfluous and without substance or meaning. His will to survive against the most extreme traumas amazed me. He had just made it out. This was all happening now.

With all this compelling imagery and little in the way of practical information, I began to plan my journey.

I have always had a close relationship with my parents—their love and care during the time of my recovery from burns had made us even closer. So, I openly discussed my plan with both my father, a college business professor, and my mother, a third-grade schoolteacher. They were sympathetic and supportive, *in principle*. But they could hardly endorse the idea of their seventeen-year-old son going halfway around the world to a war zone with no organization assuming responsibility for him. It was a better idea to go to college first, they argued, and then, with some education under my belt, I could go overseas. I accepted that they had to say this. But I was going to Thailand. And so, I resolved to continue with my plan in secret.

As I started making inquiries and calls to churches and government agencies, it rapidly became apparent that as an unskilled teenager with no Asian language abilities and no training as a medic, I was not an appealing candidate for any organization working along the Thai-Cambodian border. But I was determined, and no number of doors closing—or phones hanging up—would deter me. I kept telling myself if I can just get there, they won't turn away my help.

In spare moments at a work-study job at the advertising agency, I made calls. Long-distance calls. To Washington, D.C. To Boston. To Geneva.

I got names, addresses, and conflicting advice. Eventually, I cobbled together enough rudimentary information and a short list of potential contacts for agencies in Thailand.

I applied for a passport using an expired childhood passport as documentation. I visited the state health department for recommended vaccinations. My friend Press's mom was in on my plan. While she wasn't thrilled that I was keeping my plans from my parents, she understood that I was determined to go one way or another, so she offered me practical advice to minimize the risks and increase my chances of success at least slightly. Press and I skipped school with her for a day trip to Boston, where I applied in person for a tourist visa to Thailand at the Royal Thai Consulate. Then I emptied my bank account—slightly over $700 of what was supposed to be college money saved over three years from working summers and after school—to buy the one-way ticket and a cheap backpack. All in secret.

I kept my eye on the papers. Fighting was escalating on the border. An estimated half a million refugees were trapped between the Vietnamese and the Thai. The plight of these Cambodians was increasingly desperate.

When everything was ready, I put my plan into action.

ESCAPE

My plan was simple. I told my parents that I would spend the night at my friend Press's house, something I did often enough it did not arouse suspicion. I would launch from there.

Early the next morning, in the first light of the cold, grey, New England morning, Press and his sister Tory wished me luck, and we said our goodbyes. Press's mom gave me a ride in her Volvo station wagon into Hartford to board a Greyhound bus to New York.

"Does this bus go to JFK?" The driver nodded. Several hours later, the bus came to its final stop not at the airport, but at the Port Authority.

The Port Authority is not the airport. Now what do I do? I had no idea. Barely a baby step into my adventure and I was stopped cold in my tracks. Shit. I was wearing three velour shirts layered on top each other, no overcoat, and L.L. Bean duck boots on my feet. I was shivering. (I was smart enough to know I wouldn't need a winter coat in Thailand, but dumb enough to find myself freezing in New York).

A commuting businessman in a suit and tie recognized my distress and stopped to ask me if I needed help. He gave me directions, but they merely confused me. I thanked him and stood frozen. Another professionally dressed woman who appeared to be headed to work asked if I needed help. She suggested I take the "Train to the Plane," but recognized that I was probably too dumb to understand her instructions, so she kindly walked me a block away to the proper subway entrance.

"You'll have to hurry. You are cutting it close." As I started down the stairs to the train, she added, "You know, I ran away from home when I was seventeen." She smiled and wished me good luck.

The confusion at Port Authority had consumed valuable time. As the train started and stopped, making its slow progress towards the airport, I kept looking at my cheap blue Timex watch as I gripped the frame of my Sears backpack. The flight would leave in less than twenty minutes. When the train pulled up to JFK, I jumped the shuttle to the Pan Am terminal. I ran as fast as I could to check in to the flight.

"I'm sorry," the agent said. "That flight just pulled back from the gate. I'm afraid you missed it."

My heart was pounding, and I was out of breath from the running. For the second time that morning, I had no idea what to do. And I had a sinking feeling that my dramatic escape would soon be followed by a humiliating return home in failure. My parents surely would find me and drag me home. I'd be back in school, tail between my legs by tomorrow.

I had been told by the travel agent the ticket—a super cheap fare—was nonrefundable and could not be changed in any way. So that was it. I had just lost $550 and was stranded and broke. Defeated.

The gate attendant looked me over and I thought I detected a spark of sympathy. "You really should try to arrive at the airport earlier in the future." Her fingers clicked away on the keyboard. "Let me see what I can do." After a pause, she informed me she could get me on the next flight.

Thank God.

The flight that would leave in two days.

What? Yes! Well, yes, I'll take it.

But where would I stay? I had almost no money and no idea how to get to and from the airport, as I had just proven. I would have to wait in the terminal. Wait, as my parents—only three hours' drive away—received and read my letter. Wait, as my parents would inevitably then call the airline and learn that I had missed the flight.

I was going to get caught.

A fugitive from my own family, I spent the next forty-eight hours in the JFK Pan Am terminal in constant movement. Twice, airport security approached, having recognized me as a loiterer. Each time, I was sure they had been contacted by my parents and were coming to detain me. Would the police intervene to return a seventeen-year-old to his parents? They wouldn't… would they? The officers were merely interested in verifying that I held an outgoing ticket. Each time I produced my ticket, they moved on.

I was hungry. The one-way ticket had consumed most of my life savings. I had about seventy dollars in my pocket. I had no idea what to expect when I made it to Thailand, so I couldn't afford the high-priced airport food. I had a can of tuna I had lifted from the pantry at home in my backpack. It was supposed to sustain me if I ran into trouble in Thailand. I ate it. Once it was gone, I did not eat again for two days.

On the morning of the flight, after sleeping on the floor for two nights, I positioned myself firmly in the front and center of the boarding area. I would be the first economy passenger to board. I had only flown twice and only been overseas once to England with my parents a decade earlier. I watched nervously as the clock hands moved slowly. I needed to get on that plane.

Finally, boarding began. As I entered the cabin, I told the first attendant I saw that I had not eaten in two days. She smiled and gave me a handful of peanut packets. Meal service in an hour, she said with a smile.

I still wasn't at ease when the plane pulled back from the gate. It wasn't until the plane lifted off the runway and we were airborne that I was able to breathe a huge sigh of relief. This plane would not set down again until we arrived fourteen hours later in Tokyo.

I did it! I was on my way, and no one could stop me. By God, I did it!

The peanuts I had secured on entry to the plane had helped, but I was so relieved to see a tray with a warm meal—the first of three—placed in front of me. Pasta, chicken, and peas never tasted so good. I devoured everything that was edible on the tray. I even ate the canned pineapple. I hated canned pineapple. But I now understood I really had no idea where my meals would be coming from once I reached my destination. Better to fill up while I could.

After a two-hour layover in Tokyo, I boarded another flight to Hong Kong.

The journey from JFK to Bangkok took over thirty hours from start to finish. With each hour, I grew more hypervigilant, disoriented and sleep deprived. I was so far from home. I was halfway around the world. Even Tokyo's Narita and Hong Kong Kai Tak, though only airports, were unlike anything I had ever seen. In Hong Kong it was nighttime. I never even left the gate—too afraid I would be left behind. I stared at everything, absorbed by every passerby. Most people in these airports were Asian. I had never seen so many Asians before. I was in a whole new world.

On the last leg, the pilot came on the intercom to announce our final approach into Bangkok. We landed at Don Muang Airport twenty miles outside the city slightly after midnight, Sunday, March 9, 1980.

I was wired with jet lag and excitement the moment I walked through the door of the aircraft out onto the air stairs to the tarmac. The temperature was in the eighties and the humidity hit me like a wall. The insanely warm night air swallowed me. I struggled to catch my breath. The smell of tropical flowers intermingled with the petroleum fumes of the airport, and the lights of the small terminal were shining so brightly in the distance through the darkened night.

As I came down the air stairs from the plane to board the bus to the terminal, a uniformed policeman was scanning the disembarking passengers. He was yelling something over and over. "Passenger Allen? Passenger Allen?" My pulse stopped. As I reached the bottom steps, I approached him and nodded.

He pulled me aside. I stood, waiting in the dark, humid air next to the officer for several eternal minutes. The officer did not smile. He said nothing to me. We just waited. I was sweating. The three velour shirts that had been too cold in New York were now soaked.

They can't send me back, can they? I remember thinking. Could they arrest me this far away from home and send me back? Am I under arrest?

My senses absorbed everything. The low whisper of the idling 747 engines behind me. I had not moved any further away from the plane, but the plane seemed to move away from me. It was behind me. Whatever lay ahead lay ahead. The way the light from the terminal reflected off the wet surface of the tarmac. That warm, damp air—so late at night. The small, wiry driver of the open-air transport bus in his worn, khaki uniform as the rest of the travelers disembarked down the stairs and ran quickly across to board for the ride to the terminal. The bus pulled away. I was left behind with the officer.

FROM HIS SHORT, BLACK, brush-like military hair, to his flattened nose and tight lips, to his neck, cut close by the collar of his uniform, he was from another world. The awkwardly tight uniform, a holster, an old pistol with a worn leather strap. My eyes drifted to the bus as it drove away towards the terminal. The terminal. Would I even make it to the terminal?

Time stood still, and then he handed me a scrap of blue paper with a scrawled message on it: *"Passenger Allen/Scott. URGENT! CALL HOME IMMEDIATELY! Allen/Robert."*

My dad.

Oh no.

Maybe my abrupt departure had caused my mother to break down, or my father's ulcer to act up. My actions suggested little apparent concern for my parents' feelings—but of course I was deeply concerned about them. I had left on my journey despite my love for my family. I had been conflicted by the knowledge that my actions would cause them tremendous pain, and it would not be the first time I had caused them pain. The disbelief on my mother's face when I had come in from the yard flashed in my mind. I felt sick. I had done it to them again.

Finally, I was allowed to board another bus to the terminal, where I checked through customs and immigration and picked up my cheap Sears backpack, the last lonely piece of luggage on the carousel. I tried to ask a baggage handler where I could make a collect call. He did not speak English. I tried explaining my situation to a security officer who understood. He walked me upstairs to the post and telegraph office. Although the post office was closed for the night, a postal clerk was sleeping on a cot behind the counter. The officer woke him up, and he told me that it would cost 400 baht (roughly $20) for the first three minutes. Collect calls were not possible from this station. After brief consideration of my meager funds, I reluctantly decided the call would have to wait.

By now, a Thai taxi driver had grown attached to me. He offered to take me to Bangkok for the very cheap price of $20. After consulting the hotel information desk, I chose the airport van service instead for $2.50. I was so confused that I agreed to have the airport van service drop me off at a hotel for the night. I knew I couldn't afford it, but I was so exhausted and overwhelmed by the journey and my arrival, I could only think as far as finding a place to collapse.

The van carried about six of us, all with different destinations. I was in the front seat with the driver, my head spinning, when a man behind me said, "Where are you staying tonight?"

I turned around and there was another American, a guy, about twenty-five or thirty, wearing a brown T-shirt. He looked quite relaxed and was flipping through a book.

"Well, the lady at the airport recommended the Atlanta Hotel," I answered.

The nice Thai woman at the limo counter had quickly sized me up as a low-budget "world traveler," or WT. She had recommended a notorious, but very cheap, hotel frequented by the lost tribes of young, backpack-bearing foreigners and, as I would only later learn, known for its frequent raids and drug busts by the Thai police.

"Yes, that's supposed to be pretty good. I was going to check out the YMCA or Malaysia Hotel. My name's Richard, by the way."

"Hey, Richard. My name is Scott. How much is a room?"

"Well, you shouldn't have to pay more than three or four dollars."

"Three or four what? Dollars? No, I mean an actual room. With a lock on the door."

"Three or four dollars," he said, smiling.

With only seventy dollars left to my name, this knowledge came as a relief.

I was still petrified about figuring out what to do next. I surprised myself by asking Richard if he'd like to share a double, and he generously agreed. I was relieved. I needed some guidance, and he seemed quite at ease with the entire situation.

The van zoomed down the road at about 60 mph. We passed cyclos, bicycle carts, three-wheeled taxis, shacks, slums, and palm trees. It was two o'clock in the morning, but there were still some people on the streets, and the lights from vehicles, billboards, and signs on restaurants and businesses illuminated the city. Unbeknownst to me, there had been a *coup d'état* in Thailand only days before my arrival, and the military was in the streets flexing its muscles with military checkpoints.

The city itself was chaotic, and I felt like I was in a scene of Saigon from *The Deer Hunter*. (*The Deer Hunter* Saigon street scenes had been filmed in these very Bangkok streets only a few years earlier. No wonder they looked so familiar).

It was in the early morning hours, around three or so, when the van pulled up to the Atlanta Hotel, a plain looking unadorned four-story building tucked at the end of a lane (or *soi* in Thai). Richard and I roused the sleeping clerk from behind the desk. He informed us that the hotel was fully booked. No rooms. It was the middle of the night and the van had departed, so Richard begged the clerk to allow us to sleep somewhere for the night, even in the lobby if need be. The clerk nodded, and after filling out detailed registration cards and having them checked against our passports, he led us up three flights of stairs to a room that literally had a hole in the wall large enough to crawl in and out of because it was under repair. Richard and I looked at each other quizzically. But we were both dog tired. This unfinished and unsecured room would have to do.

We entered the hot, humid room. There was a sultry breeze through the open windows. Palm trees swayed above a picturesque courtyard pool. Richard got the ceiling fan going, but it merely pushed the muggy air around. My brain was on overload. I collapsed on the hard cot and fell fast asleep.

BANGKOK

The next morning, Bangkok presented herself in all her splendor, wonder, hustle, bustle, and vibrancy. I might as well have been on another planet. Richard and I walked down the untidy and broken *soi* from the Atlanta Hotel past muddy gutters, small plastic baskets of rotting refuse, abandoned lots occupied by squatters in makeshift shelters, a multitude of small roadside vendors with their carts of noodle soup and fried dough. Past their little folding tables with their cups of chili and vinegar, and little red metal stools that were bent and broken and then hammered back into service, among the strange, new, and pungent smells of a whole new vocabulary of food. Towards the increasingly loud rumble and buzz of the busy main street of Sukhumvit Road, with the whine of armies of motorcycles and the sputter of three-wheeled taxis known as *tuk-tuks*, and the nasally meandering melody lines of the popular Thai songs that blared from tinny loudspeakers.

We rounded the corner, ducking away from an aggressive and desperate taxi driver who haggled with us for a ride we had not requested until we finally broke away into a small storefront restaurant for a quick and desperately needed bottle of Coke—a drink that despite its recent refrigeration seemed to far too rapidly achieve ambient temperature in the time it took me to suck it down. We squeezed past the delicate woman with long, black hair and colorful wraparound sarongs who had placed her wares of cheaply made shirts out on a torn piece of cardboard as she called out in the singsong words of the Thai language.

We hastily jumped aboard one of the overloaded blue and white open buses of the Bangkok Transit Authority, buses that came two or three deep, with young men hanging off the front and back door by tenuous grip. Up, into the throng, in the heat, with the smell of sweat, as the bus conductors, young thin men in blue pants with thin white shirts that contrasted against their golden-brown skin, chattered and clicked their cylindrical tin boxes full of thin paper tear-off tickets and tarnished silver baht and copper satang coins, while they never forgot who had paid and who had not. We rocked and bumped, hanging from the ceiling grab bar as the warm, humid air, full of fuel and smog and rot and cooking food blew by our faces, as the shop buildings and busy sidewalks and clusters of food stalls and fruit stands drifted by, as we crossed bridges over the dank greenish brown water of the *klongs*, the city's waterways. Bangkok had absorbed me, and as I slowly transformed to a small particle in the cosmic whirlwind of the Asian city, I was in a state of utter amazement and culture shock. And I was thrilled.

The day flew by in a blur. My senses primed, I focused intensely on every detail, from the chatter of sidewalk vendors to the strange sights and smells of exotic fruits and spicy foods, to the clusters of schoolchildren with their navy-blue pleated skirts and shorts and their crisp white shirts, to the poise and grace that governed the movements of the older pedestrians as they went about their business. From the prattle and rumbling of engines large and small, to the sea of billboards and signs, many hand painted with slight distortions of the images, and the unfamiliar Thai characters that hawked sometimes familiar products like Coke and Sony Electronics. From the clusters of disenfranchised, poor city dwellers who had taken to squatting in various crevices and overhangs, to the broken, uneven, and interrupted sagging sidewalks.

The people almost invariably greeted us with a smile as we tended to what little business and shopping we could accomplish on a Sunday, and secured ourselves a more suitable room in the slightly less tourist-burdened Star Hotel at Siam Square.

Richard had been to Bangkok before and he showed me around the low budget "world traveler" ghettos of the Atlanta Hotel, and the Malaysia. We moved easily among the European and Australian thong-sandaled backpacking travelers. The Doors "Hello, I Love You" played over the open-air coffee shop jukebox. I had found the lost children of the sixties. There they were, in Bangkok of 1980, turning on, tuning in, and dropping out.

Bulletin boards in the lobbies of the Atlanta were layered thick by messages, spontaneously written travel advice: "Watch out for TK Travel—they ripped us off on train tickets." "Traveling on to Kuala Lumpur—looking for company." Enterprising and independent travel agents and touts in the lobby peddled fake international driving permits, student I.D.s, and offers to arrange any sort of travel or adventure or perhaps a massage: "You like massage?"

I was struck by the different pace and flow of life in Thailand. Despite its bustle and confusion, even Bangkok moved with less anxiety than the world I had left. There was a grace and detachment that characterized the way business was conducted. There was rush, and yet there was never any hurry. There were fast-paced moments, and yet there was no urgency. Things proceeded in their own time, at their own pace.

As my first full day in Thailand was Sunday, all administrative offices were closed.

Monday, my second full day in the Kingdom, was the first opportunity I would have to try to contact my parents from the phone banks at the General Post Office. By now, Richard had heard my story, and he understood the importance of getting through to my family to reassure them that I had arrived and I was well. He accompanied me across town to the General Post Office.

To pass the hour-long wait for our turn at the phone, we chatted with several other world travelers. One, a seemingly well-informed

Australian man with a reddish blonde beard and a thin, worn face, asked what our plans were. Richard spoke of his plans to travel outside Bangkok, and then slowly, over the next six months, to work his way country by country from Thailand to Malaysia to Indonesia, to Nepal and India, and on and on until he eventually reached Europe and then home again. I told him I hoped to find work in the border camps.

"Well," the Aussie said with eminent authority, "you're a bit late for that. I was up at Sakeo in the early days. Bloody mess it was. But before long, with the flood of world attention, the camp was overrun by relief agencies, church groups, and UN staff. They were stepping all over each other. They were turning volunteers away by the end of the first week."

My heart sank. Had I come all this way for nothing?

THE CALL HOME

The Thai operator at the General Post Office called my name. "I have Mr. Robert Allen for Mr. Scott Allen."

I scurried into the old wood-framed phone booth and lifted the heavy red receiver to my ear.

"Hello?" I said nervously. "Hello?" echoed my own voice on the line. Then a pause.

"Scott? This is Dad." The familiar voice of my father was distant.

Then my father said, "We will talk later about how you left, but now that you are there, we want you to do what you went there to do."

Except for my departure note, they had not heard from me. Five days had passed. Then, a collect call from Thailand. That first awkward call, patched by hand by a Thai telephone exchange worker to a small booth on a tenuous echo-burdened line, lasted less than five minutes and cost my parents a small fortune.

Dad told me how they had called Pan Am overwhelmed with worry to see if I had made my original flight two days after my departure because my note had said I would contact them from Bangkok as soon as I arrived—and well, I should have already arrived. The Pan Am representative informed them I hadn't boarded the original flight.

But I did board the one that left two days later, a mere half hour or so before their call. They had come that close to stopping me.

It was a welcome relief to hear that my parents were willing to set aside my behavior for the moment and were in support of my ultimate plans. It meant a great deal to me.

My father told me he had been in touch with the US embassy in Bangkok. He advised me to go see a Mr. Zajac as he might be able to help me find a volunteer job. This was encouraging, coming so soon after the pessimistic opinions of my Australian acquaintance.

On Monday, I reported to the US embassy and was admitted into the compound to meet Consular Officer Eugene Zajac.

"Your dad says you're a good kid and we should give you a chance."

The following day, I reported to the US Embassy Refugee Section, a short distance from the main US embassy on Wireless Road. There, as had previously been arranged by Mr. Zajac, I met up with David Lewis. David was a career volunteer agency man, having become involved with international relief work during the Vietnam War when he had earlier served in the military. He now headed up the in-country relief work for the US contingent of the International Catholic Migration Commission (ICMC) in cooperation with the Thai affiliate, Catholic Office for Emergency Relief to Refugees (COERR).

David was an affable, easily distractible man with curly brown hair and mustache and a slight middle-aged weariness betrayed by a loss of definition to his body and face. He wore the informal "diplomat casual" attire that was popular in Thailand those days: a safari suit consisting of an untucked hip length shirt with epaulettes and four pockets with matching slacks, the kind of thing the cheap Indian tailors of Sukhumvit would knock off overnight. He seemed not to have a fixed itinerary or plan, jumping from moment to moment, a personality trait that at the same time made him ideal in a fast-changing refugee relief environment that would tax all those around him. I was later to learn he was divorced, but I might have guessed his unattached condition by the way he lingered in an awkward flirtation with the attractive Thai secretary in the Refugee Section office where we first met.

After a few brief calls on Refugee Section associates, David led me to his chauffeur-driven white Mercedes, and as we sat in the back, I saw Bangkok from a very different point of view—the quiet and comfort of an air-conditioned luxury car. I thought it odd for a relief agency official to be in a chauffeur-driven Mercedes, but then, everything seemed odd to me at this point.

I was driven to his comfortable rented home on a sub-*soi* off upper Sukhumvit Soi 63. The housekeeper served a lunch of soup, curry, and fresh fruit. David explained that he had plenty of volunteers that had loads of experience—doctors, nurses, and other professionals—but he didn't have enough *non-professionals*. He had no foot soldiers. When setting up teams for the camps, everyone wanted to run things, no one wanted to do the grunt work. He said he could offer me a chance to join a new team headed to Mai Rut (pronounced "*my root*") camp. The rest of the team would arrive from the states in coming days.

"So, yes, I think I can use you."

He was being kind. Even I knew I obviously had little or nothing practical to offer anyone.

"These people are special," he told me. David had first come to Southeast Asia as a soldier in Vietnam, but he returned after his tour to work with relief agencies helping people displaced by the war. He had even married a Vietnamese woman, but it had not worked out. In his mid- to late forties, David looked a little worn out for his age, as if things had not gone as he had hoped.

"The Cambodians, the Vietnamese, the Laotians, the Thai—they are all unique and fascinating. Once you get to know them, you'll see—they'll get under your skin. Once they do, you'll never leave them."

David continued to chew his food, momentarily lost in thought. He was looking out the window into the sky above Bangkok when he sighed. "This work can wear you out."

As he regained his focus, he warned me of the dangers. Combat near the camps was rare but an ever-present threat. The border was heavily mined and often shelled. More likely, though, I would get sick from malarial insect bites or from something I ate. The agency would provide pills for malaria prevention, but the pills themselves could make you sick too. Traveler's diarrhea was a given, the price of admission to the foreign visitor in Southeast Asia.

Mai Rut, he explained, is down near the southern end of the Thai-Cambodian border on the Gulf of Siam. There were two thousand people in our section of the camp, including Khmer Serei (Free Khmer—a non-communist group) and Chinese Khmer. Khmer is what Cambodians call themselves. However, within six weeks, the Thai military planned to move in as many as twenty thousand refugees from further north on the border. It could become one of the major refugee camps in Thailand.

For my contributions, I would get room and board and twenty-five dollars a week in the local currency.

David's offer could not have come at a better time. Despite the low cost of living, my money, after only five days in Thailand, was gone. As I rose to leave, I hesitated and stood there awkwardly.

"You don't have any money, do you?" he asked.

He reached for his wallet and handed me a 500-baht bill as he put me in the Mercedes to be driven back to my hotel.

Back at the hotel, I reflected on my good fortune. I had always realized that my scheme of getting to the border was a bit harebrained, but it seemed like it was working. The series of unlikely events that colluded to keep me on track only served to reinforce my belief that this journey was meant to be.

When David described the dangers of the border, which were consistent with what I had read, it did give me pause. Despite my compulsion to go where I was going, I was not a thrill seeker. Danger did not appeal to me. I had no romantic notions of heroism, nor any sense that I could save anybody. But if there was that much human suffering in one place, I was drawn to it. I was moving back into the heart of darkness, yet somehow, I felt like I was going home.

On Sunday, a full week after arriving in Thailand and after much anticipation, I finally made the trip from Bangkok to Trat, southeast of Bangkok and approximately six hours by car. The countryside of Thailand was so different from the city, with its wide-open rice paddies dotted with water buffalo and small roadside stands selling sodas, fruit, and fried rice. I traveled with Mai, an attractive and delicate appearing young Vietnamese woman, maybe in her mid-twenties, who worked as an assistant to David. Mai had been a refugee herself in 1975, and initially resettled in Australia. She had returned to Southeast Asia and had found work in the refugee relief effort. Already fluent in Vietnamese, French, and English, she picked up Thai as a new language and spoke it fluently. Her fragile physical appearance was deceptive. This woman clearly knew how to survive anywhere, and she took charge of me without hesitation.

We arrived in Trat in the evening. Mai assisted me in checking in to my room at the Trat Hotel overlooking the open market. This was the major hotel in this small provincial capital: a quirky three-story cement structure with gates that closed at night to protect guest cars parked in the central courtyard.

That evening, Mai invited me to join her at the home of some Thai friends she had made since she had first come to Trat. Her friends lived outside of Trat in a rural rice farming area. Although it was only a few miles from the center of town, in the dark of night and the open air of the rice fields, it seemed so far away. Their home was a traditional Thai home constructed of wood and thatch and elevated from the surrounding rice paddies on stilts. It had an open structure so that as you sat on the wooden floor, the breeze from the rice paddy blew softly through the home. The Thai leave their shoes at the door, and, not for the last time, I struggled to unlace my L.L Bean boots (what was I thinking?) as we entered the home.

Not one of her Thai friends spoke a word of English, but the family welcomed me warmly. The family was large, with four or five sons in their teens and twenties, all well-conditioned from their manual work in the rice fields. We sat cross-legged on the worn, smooth, wood floor, eating rice and curry, with Mai interpreting and the family enthusiastically teaching me my first Thai words. As the evening progressed, they sent one of the sons out to purchase bottles of Singha beer, a potent Thai brew. We drank, talked, and laughed. As the beer worked its inevitable way through my system, I found myself with the pressing need to learn the Thai word for "toilet." Following this rather rushed language lesson, I found myself teetering above an Asian-style squat toilet trying not to pee on myself. I knew I was far from home. I struggled to solve the puzzle of the operation and flushing of this most basic and simple facility in my hazy state of mind. Ah, scoop the water from the cistern and dump it into the toilet!

As I returned to the gathering, I was inebriated and happy. I distinctly remember laughing heartily at a joke that someone made. We all were laughing together, and I remember thinking, Wait! I don't speak Thai. Why am I laughing? I don't understand a word he said. Without further thought, I lapsed back into the incoherence of the alcohol.

This was beyond anything I could ever have imagined. The intoxication was more than just the alcohol. It was the entire experience. I felt a sense of incredible freedom. From the house, I could look out into the wide-open sky. I was half a world away from everything I had ever known. I was with complete strangers, and yet I was safe and warm.

The following day, I would meet the rest of the team and head down to the small Cambodian border camp of Mairut. I had to sober up. And when I did, my sense of wonder and excitement had not abated. I had no alarm clock, but I was awake with the morning light. Today, I would arrive at my destination. The Cambodian border. Things were about to get real.

THE CAMBODIAN BORDER

The morning after my night out with Mai, I met two Austrian nurses and an Italian doctor, the first members of the COERR Mairut team, in the lobby of the Trat Hotel. The Italian doctor sat apart from the rest of the team on the heavy and uncomfortable wooden furniture, and she seemed to not want to associate with us. The older of the two nurses was a serious woman whose very demeanor underscored the gravity of her work. She was contrasted by the warmness of her compatriot, an attractive dark-haired woman with an amiable smile. The younger nurse welcomed me warmly. The older one looked me up and down and said in her crisp Austrian accent, "We ask David to send us a man so the woman could feel more secure. So, he sends a boy."

We were expecting four nuns from the order of the Sisters of Mercy from New York, but they had not yet arrived in town, so for now, the team was made up of the four of us, the driver, and Mai. When our driver arrived, we climbed aboard the small blue Japanese van and headed off south on the main road from the Trat provincial city towards Khlong Yai on the southernmost strip of the Thai-Cambodian border.

The road south ran between the wide-open gulf of Siam, with an endless ribbon of rice paddies separating the road and the ocean to the west, and the edge of the Cardamom Mountains, the geographic border with Cambodia, which at times was just yards away from the driver's side of the van. The mountains were thick with jungle vegetation, and as we made the hour-long ride for the first time, I stared into the deep impenetrable thicket, wondering if and where Khmer Rouge soldiers might be hiding, and what was transpiring beyond the boundaries of the still isolated and darkened country of Cambodia, so close that I could touch it, and yet still as impassable and unknowable as it had been when I was at home in America.

We passed several military checkpoints on the way, with their red and white wooden gates balanced with sandbag counterweights and sandbag bunkers manned by young Thai soldiers in combat greens and helmets. With each kilometer traveled, we were moving deeper into a military zone where access was restricted. I had seen soldiers with machine guns in pictures and movies, but this was real. I was really here.

Thai farmers worked the rice fields to the right, with the aid of large, lumbering gray water buffalo. The horizon of the ocean seemed an infinite distance away. To the left, rising up steeply, was the teeming and verdant mountain forest.

We passed the Queen's Camp, a picturesque seaside village of durably constructed thick, thatch-roofed buildings, with large red crosses on white backgrounds on each roof that were meant to discourage shelling from either the Khmer Rouge or Vietnamese.

"This is a show camp," Mai explained. "It was created at the queen's request to house and care for the growing number of orphans and unaccompanied minors who are arriving on the border every day. But it is mostly here for show. None of the other camps look as nice."

After nearly an hour, we came into view of Mairut Camp, the southernmost refugee camp on the Thai-Cambodian border. From the road, we could see two low-lying camps set back from the beach bluff: the "Old Camp" and the "Bamboo Camp." The Old Camp was a weary looking graying camp with wooden barracks ringed with double rows of barbed wire. It had opened in 1976 according to Mai. It housed about three thousand of the first refugees from the Pol Pot regime who were ironically Khmer Rouge cadre ousted in purges. The other camp was clearly newer, the bamboo and thatch barracks still gleaming and clean, white sand on the short flat expanse that ran between the border's mountain-hugging road and the gleaming gulf of Siam. It housed another three thousand new arrivals. Finally, a small military base with a central courtyard, wooden barracks, and a raised main office where a pole ringed by white stone flew the Thai flag occupied the space between the Old Camp and the Bamboo Camp.

As we turned onto the bumpy dirt road heading into the camp, we were stopped by soldiers in olive uniforms and black boots, worn M-16 rifles slung casually over their shoulders. The driver showed them our passes issued by the Thai Ministry of the Interior. One soldier poked his head in the driver's side window and looked at each of us. After some inquiries handled by Mai and our driver, we were allowed to proceed.

As we drew nearer to the Old Camp, I looked at the wooden and bamboo structures. There were black pajamas hanging from lines strung between barracks. Remarkably, in the white sands, green vegetables were growing. "They use sewage for fertilizer" someone said, and whether that was true or not, it amazed me that anyone could grow anything on a beach.

Then I saw the people. Cambodians of the Old Camp. They wore the black pajamas, black rubber tire sandals, and red-and-white-checkered scarves, or *khramas*.

"Khmer Rouge," Mai said. Cambodian communists. As the van slowly made its way down the bumpy road, a few stared back, dark eyes lighted by fleeting curiosity.

We pulled up to a small, beautifully ornate temple-like hut made of bamboo marked by the pale blue-and-white flag of the United Nations. Mai explained that this was the headquarters of the United Nations High Commissioner for Refugees (UNHCR), the agency charged with coordinating all the volunteer agencies involved in relief efforts in the camp. As we climbed out of the van, I stood and stretched in the bright, hot sun, and with squinting eyes, looked all around: first towards the nearby Old Camp where people were quietly going about their business, then over the bluff towards the waters of the Gulf of Siam, and finally towards the distant Bamboo Camp, the newest expansion with the newest refugees. It was sunny and hot, but the breeze off the ocean was refreshing. The light and openness were not at all what I had been expecting in a refugee camp. Indeed, unlike the inland border camps to the north, Mairut was in some ways located in an idyllic setting.

A radiant and effusive Thai UNHCR staffer named Dang emerged from the UNHCR hut and welcomed us. Dang would become my first Thai friend, and in the coming days and months she would take me under her wing. She invited us into the hut to get out of the sun.

"Are you David's son?" Dang asked.

"Um, no. My name is Scott. I'm a volunteer. I'm here to work."

She smiled warmly, and I immediately knew I liked her. Dang was in her early thirties and, I would later learn, from a prominent family who she kept in the dark about her work as they would not have approved of her being in such a remote and dangerous post. She had an infectious energy and seemed to always be positive whatever the challenges at hand. With short black hair and a broad smile, she was in constant motion, jumping from point to point in the camp and from person to person, deftly smoothing over the wrinkles and minor conflicts that inevitably arose from international refugee relief work.

The UNHCR hut was a small, four-room structure, with a receiving area with Dang's desk and a storage room in the front, and the radio room and the field coordinator's office in the back. In the radio room, the tall, affable Norwegian radio man was tapping out outgoing messages to Bangkok in Morse code. Dang interrupted him long enough for us to exchange pleasant smiles and greetings. Just then, a jeep pulled up, driven by another Thai UN staffer and carrying Stephan Lahusen, a lanky, twenty-six-year-old German who was the UN field coordinator. Stephan had only recently arrived, along with the new residents of the Bamboo Camp from Sakeo Camp up north.

Just by the way he carried himself with purpose and seriousness, and the way he wore his khaki UN uniform, I could tell he was important.

Soon, David Lewis arrived in his Mercedes, having spent the night in the more comfortable westernized hotel in Chanthaburi, two hours to the north.

David sat me down with Stephan and summarized my situation.

"I'm not sure what use you can make of him," David said, "but as far as COERR is concerned, you can use him to fill in and help out with any of the agencies here in camp."

Stephan, a reserved, soft-spoken man with an easygoing smile and light brown hair, expressed his appreciation for David's generosity (for as I was to learn, the division of labor and assignment among the various agencies was a source of great friction to the point of turf wars). Still, even I had no idea what role I could play.

Stephan invited us to join the weekly UNHCR meeting, and workers from the other voluntary agencies—called "Volags"—began to arrive and take places in the chairs lining the wall in Stephan's office. He introduced me to the other relief workers, and they greeted me politely.

French doctors and nurses of Medicines Sans Frontieres (MSF) staffed the camp hospital. The supplementary feeding unit was the provision of the young and bright Irish women of CONCERN. Two industrious missionary workers from the Southern Baptist Church in the United States oversaw a variety of programs in the Old Camp. A middle-aged American public health worker attached to the UNHCR rounded out the team. For a border camp, this was a very small contingent of international workers. This, I was to learn, was an advantage, as the camaraderie afforded by our small size was atypical of the larger camps to the north. Still, I struggled to learn all the acronyms, names, and roles of the various relief agencies and workers that flowed so easily from everyone's mouths.

Children lingered by the open window and looked on as Stephan called the meeting to order. "I will need COERR in the Bamboo Camp. Presently, there are about two thousand new arrivals, mostly Chinese Khmer and Khmer Serei moved down from Sakeo. COERR will provide the outpatient clinic (or OPD for outpatient department in Volag jargon), and an OPD building needs to be constructed."

"I have four nuns due to arrive imminently," David said. "Perhaps they could set up a sewing center."

"That would be fine." Stephan had a low-key style, one that had served him well in the daily challenges of serving as coordinator and liaison between a variety of strong-minded individuals with often conflicting agendas complicated by cross-cultural barriers.

A Thai lieutenant from the local military command arrived to review security matters. He was a military man, stiff and formal. A nurse from CONCERN expressed unease with the fact that the camp guards carried loaded M-16s with the safety off around children. She expressed her opinion loudly and with genuine emotional intensity. There had already been an accidental shooting of a volunteer nun in the town of Aranyaprathet when a soldier was cleaning his rifle. The lieutenant stiffened as she spoke.

"You are in a combat zone," was all he said in reply.

There was discussion about fighting and shelling in camps slightly to the north in recent days. An Irish nurse from CONCERN asked about an evacuation plan for the workers and the refugees in the event of artillery fire on Mairut. This seemed to trigger the Italian doctor, who already appeared irritable even before the meeting started.

"Further north on the border, when the camps are shelled, everyone flees deeper into Thailand. What are we going to do here? Swim into the gulf?" she asked.

The lack of an evacuation plan was acknowledged, and Stephan and the officer said they would take that issue up with the camp commander, Colonel Kosol, at the earliest opportunity.

"But you don't need to worry," the lieutenant assured. "We will keep you safe here."

Nobody seemed assured, least of all the Italian doctor. She outright sneered at the lieutenant. (She would be kicked out of the camp by the military within the week. Her demeanor and directness did not mix well with the local Thai norms and customs).

The situation on the southern border was chaotic. David had

explained this all to me in Bangkok before my departure. On a relatively narrow strip of mountains, a confusing assortment of rebels and armies vied for control. Making up the western defensive line were the Thai military, with regular forces and tank divisions to the north, and a more roguish, ragtag unit of Thai irregulars known as Task Force 80 running the show on the front line of the border. In the middle were the camps in two basic groups: those on the Thai side of the border, and those straddling the border or in the Cambodian interior. The border camps were run by a tenuous collaboration between the Thai forces and local Cambodian rebel factions, which included the bulk of the fleeing Khmer Rouge forces, and smaller numbers of non-communist rebels, including the Khmer People's National Liberation Front (KPNLF), plus forces farther north loyal to Norodom Sihanouk. The last and perhaps largest force was the Vietnamese army, who had overthrown the Khmer Rouge with a decisive invasion the previous year. Although the Khmer forces were limited to small arms and small artillery, both the Thai and the Vietnamese had heavy artillery facing each other, and shelling both ways was a regular part of border life.

The discussion continued and I tried to keep up, but there was so much to take in and my mind grew cloudy. It was hard to process that, a little over a week after closing a book in a high school classroom, I was in a refugee camp in a war zone talking about guns, shelling, and evacuation plans. I knew I had a lot to learn, and I would need to learn quickly.

Following the security discussion, Stephan adjourned the meeting. I rejoined the COERR team, and we re-boarded the van for the short ride over to the Bamboo Camp.

"Oh, by the way," David said to me as he and Mai prepared to depart back to Bangkok, "don't wander outside the camp. There are landmines everywhere."

MAIRUT CAMP

I had finally arrived at my destination. I was focused and determined but also unsure of what I was supposed to do next. The fact that I was young, inexperienced, and unqualified to be in that place at that time was beginning to reveal itself. In all the thinking and planning I had done in anticipation of getting to the border, I had never thought clearly through to this moment. I'm here. Now what?

As we approached the gate to Bamboo Camp, I surveyed the area. The camp was on flat white sandy ground set back from the ocean bluff. It was surrounded by barbed wire and patrolled by young armed Thai soldiers. There was a wooden guardhouse by the main gate and occasionally the two-way radio inside would crackle with indecipherable Thai words. Small barefoot children in ragged donated clothing were clinging to the barbed wire, hands delicately placed between the pointy barbs on the fences that surrounded rows and rows of thatch and bamboo refugee barracks. They watched us intently as we approached.

The bright white sand accentuated the honey brown skin of the children. As we drew nearer, they jumped up and down shouting, "Okay-bye-bye! Okay-bye-bye!"—a chant made up of the only English words they knew. Slightly older children (only nine or ten years old) held babies one-armed on their hips. A few older men and women wandered nearer to look at us. The Cambodians in the Bamboo Camp were thin, but not starving. They smiled. They didn't frown or look sad or burdened.

It was all more serene than I had expected.

It was midmorning, and the sun was growing hotter. It was hotter and brighter than anything I had ever experienced; I had to squint just to see. The team stepped into the shade of a small building housing the temporary outpatient clinic and I followed. The two Austrian nurses and the Italian doctor went about inspecting the temporary makeshift medical space and started unpacking newly delivered medical supplies onto a small shelf. I watched them and I offered to help, but they said they were fine. After a few moments of me lingering awkwardly, the younger nurse turned to me.

"Why don't you take a walk around the camp to get acclimated?"

Clearly, no one had figured out what I could do to help yet.

I started walking into the camp with no idea of where I was going or what I might find. I was way out of my element. I might as well have been on the moon.

As I meandered through the rows of bamboo barracks with their low-slung thatched roofs, the Cambodian people who lived here stopped and stared. I knew that an American was probably not a common sight—especially not one my age—but it felt strange to be the object of such curiosity. I smiled awkwardly. They smiled back. I walked down the path that ran between two rows of bamboo barracks. Then an unexpected object caught my eye. In the ground, sticking out of the sand, about eight inches high, was a little plastic sign with the familiar golden arches of McDonald's. As I stopped to wonder at this little curiosity, I was approached by a smiling man in a white button-down shirt and blue jeans and thong sandals who had emerged from one of the bamboo barracks.

"Greetings. Welcome to Mairut Camp. My name is Ly. I'm very happy to meet you."

I reached out and shook the hand of the first Cambodian I had ever met. I introduced myself, and Ly struggled with the correct pronunciation of my name.

"Well, do you like my sign?" he asked.

I laughed and said, "Yes. Do you know what that sign is?"

"Well, I am not sure. It came with some toys they sent for the children. I put it there for fun." He smiled. "Come. Would you like to look around? Not many people here speak any English, but I do speak some. I can interpret for you." I nodded in the affirmative and thanked him, and we waded into the crowd that had formed in the brief first minutes of my arrival. I was excited to make a connection and gratified to have Ly's help as a translator.

"Where are you from?" Ly inquired.

"I am from the United States. America."

"Oh, well, you have come very far. But, you know, we are so glad to see you here. We are grateful for the Americans and hope that you can help us."

Ly was a thin man in his early thirties with a mop of jet-black hair and twinkling eyes, and a few prominent strands of beard protruding from his otherwise hairless chin. He had an easy way about him, and he walked me through the camp as more and more curious people emerged from the sun shelter of the barracks to see what the cause for commotion was.

The way the Cambodian residents of the Mairut Holding Center Bamboo Camp welcomed me surprised me. Even more amazing to me than their warmth and smiles was a palpable spirit of optimism and maybe even the relief they exuded. I must admit, having heard of their desperate condition, I expected to see a broken and miserable lot. I could not have been more incorrect. I was meeting a group of Cambodians who had suffered greatly under the Khmer Rouge nightmare at the very moment of their escape to relative freedom and safety. Their futures were never more uncertain, but here, they were relatively free of the despotism and terror. They were, for a fragile moment, relatively secure. They could interact with each other without constant fear of punishment or torture. They could dream. They were living day to day and yet, for the first time in years, they could reach beyond the next day. Their sense of relief was striking to me. They were still on the front line of a war zone. I and my fellow relief workers were on edge concerning the safety and security of the camp. To them, that was a small price to pay for survival. Although it was unexpected, something about this felt right to me. The peace one feels living just this side of death. That moment that comes after the fire.

Ly walked me around the long, low bamboo and thatch barracks, all numbered, that were overflowing with people who were wise enough to seek shelter from the oppressively blistering midday sun that reflected blindingly off the white sand.

As we talked to people, with Ly skillfully interpreting every comment and question, the energy, eagerness, and friendliness of the Cambodians washed over me. Many of them were still wearing the pants of the black pajama uniforms and rubber tire sandals favored by the deposed Khmer Rouge regime. More and more refugees in the new Bamboo Camp came up to greet me as Ly and I made our way slowly, staring at me with amusement and curiosity, making timid and polite inquiries of me through Ly. "Who are you? Where are you from? Why are you here?"

They were so friendly, so gentle. They smiled warmly and nodded as I walked through the camp with Ly. Most of the people were from the countryside, from small villages, Ly explained. Most of them had never been outside of Cambodia, or even to a big city, nor had they met Americans before coming to the border.

As we walked along the barbed wire fence, followed by a small and curious crowd, an elderly Cambodian man walked up to me, reached out and stroked my chin, and then said something in Khmer (the language of the Cambodian or Khmer people) and everyone burst out laughing.

I felt my face flush with embarrassment and looked to Ly for an explanation.

"Well, the man said, 'You all are waiting for the Americans to save us. Look here. They sent this boy who is too young to even shave!'"

After a short walk around the camp, Ly brought me back to Building 19, a low, long bamboo building in the middle of rows of similar buildings that were divided into small living units and filled past capacity with refugees. The end of the building that opened onto the middle path by the latrines was his temporary home.

As we entered, Ly introduced me to his wife, Kolap. Kolap was a short woman in a simple T-shirt and a brightly colored sarong with thick wavy black hair and a bright smile. She gestured for me to sit, and then barked orders for one of the children to fetch me some weak tea to drink, a gesture that was deeply appreciated as my body, only a week out of the New England winter, was rapidly becoming dehydrated in the baking hot sun.

Then, only moments after I sat down, another woman who had been sitting nearby grabbed my hand assertively and pulled me over to sit down next to her. I had not expected this. I was caught off guard. Although I had only been in Asia for a week, I had observed that the people were very respectful and reserved. Her touch was most unexpected. I wasn't sure how to respond.

She appeared to be roughly the same age as Ly and Kolap. Attractive in a natural and effortless way, she wore a light blue short-sleeved top and a yellow, turquoise, and gold sarong wrapped around her waist.

She tapped a book on her lap and looked up at me expectantly.

Ly laughed.

"This is Thida, our friend. I think she wants you to help her with her English." Although Thida (pronounce *Tee-dah*) could not speak English, she had made it abundantly clear that ours was not going to be just a passing acquaintance. She emphatically moved the fingers of her free hand across the pages of a ragged English primer, while I helped her with her hesitant and awkward pronunciation. Despite the boldness of her move, she kept her eyes on the book, too shy for the moment to look me in the eye. But she held tight to my hand. She sat to my right, so it was my burned and deformed hand that she held. The gentle wave of black shoulder-length hair partially obscured her face as she looked down at her book. I had not been in the camp for an hour, and here I sat, with a woman tightly holding on to me. I was flattered by her attention, but also unsure of how I would free myself. I was beginning to feel like everyone wanted something from me—needed something from me—and I was not wrong. The crowd of onlookers outside Ly's barracks was growing, and others were pressing Ly to speak with me.

Overwhelmed by the crowd, I focused on Thida. While her tight grip had startled me, something about her soon calmed me. Already, people in the crowd were competing for my attention. My arrival was creating quite a stir. But there was something in Thida's eyes when she would briefly look at me, and in the way she pulled me close to her side. She was much older than me, but I immediately felt an attraction to her. As I sat so close to her, I could smell her scent, mixed with the mentholated smell of Tiger Balm, all mixed with the smells of human sweat in the midday tropical heat and cramped quarters. Thida was nervous, but so was I. She was also determined that I would not leave her. Her desperation drew me in like bait. She continued to grip my hand with her left hand as she traced the words in her book with her right. She tapped the book and looked at me.

"That says 'I will go to the store on Saturday.'"

"I-will-go-to-the-store-on-Sa-Tur-Day ..." she said in a very soft voice.

She would not let go of my hand. She insisted on having me read several more pages of her book while she repeated the words I read aloud. I began to wonder how long this could continue. I had no idea how to handle the situation, and I made a pleading glance towards Ly.

Ly intervened in his gentle and diplomatic way, saying something to her in Khmer. Thida smiled and said thank you, finally letting go of my hand. She quietly withdrew to another corner of the small living space. But if her goal was to lay claim to me, to be noticed among the masses, she had succeeded.

"I think she really wants to know you," Ly explained. "She is alone with her seven children and has no other family to help her."

I wanted to know her too. I was intrigued by her and drawn to her for reasons I did not understand. It was clear to me from that first encounter, though, that any relationship would not be casual. Here, everything was high stakes and her desperation—her need—was obvious. But I also was attracted to her, and not in a sexual or romantic way. I was attracted to an aura about her, something comforting, something that seemed to be good and positive that I could not explain. If her bold, nonverbal approach was a wild gamble to connect with me, it had definitely worked. We had bonded. I had been in the camp for less than an hour.

The thatch barracks were divided long ways in half, and then divided further into four or five sections. Each unit was about ten by twelve feet. Since the initial construction, the refugees had secured small amounts of additional bamboo, and the more enterprising had begun to adorn and personalize their living spaces. Ly, the eternally optimistic and enterprising survivor, had developed his living area the most. First, he made a raised bamboo platform within the living area that served by night as a bed and by day as a raised living, sitting, and dining area. At its low point of about five feet, the edge of the roof was so close to the ground that one had to duck to enter the living area. Outside, he added a canopy under which he had constructed a bench. The bench accommodated guests, and at other times served as the food preparation area. The women cooked food on small charcoal fires in clay pots, cheap tin pots, and dented woks. They washed clothes and dishes and utensils by hand in red and blue plastic buckets that had been provided by the UN and clotheslines were strung like flag-bearing spider webs in between the narrow rows that divided the barrack buildings.

This modest dwelling, and the small corner assigned to the families of Ly and Thida, would become my home away from home for the days and months that followed. It was on Ly's bench that I would sit for hours as various residents of the camp would come by and, with the gracious assistance of Ly's bilingual abilities, unburden themselves of the stories of suffering and survival. Their stories were followed by endless inquiry and consultation regarding life in the Western world, the extent of knowledge and awareness in the free world concerning the fate of the Cambodian victims of the Khmer Rouge, and advice on securing desperately sought-after resettlement in a Western country such as France or the US.

Whether or not I realized it, I was serving as a witness. As an audience. As a validator of everything the Cambodians had endured. I was there to hear and recognize their stories. At seventeen years old, I was one of the first outsiders these survivors of the killing fields of the Pol Pot regime shared their survival stories with. The fact that I had so little work to do only made me more available and approachable to the refugees who wanted to unburden themselves by the recounting of their individual traumatic survival stories.

In between the rows of barracks were latrines and open wells. The latrines were prefabricated units designed in the Western style such that the doors were eighteen inches off the ground. The problem was that the toilets within were the Asian squat style toilets. Squatting in such a latrine would expose one's private areas, so the refugees had added makeshift attachments of thatch and cardboard to the lower edges of the door.

Outside of the latrines, there was absolutely no privacy. At home, I had a bedroom to myself and never thought much of it. Here, ten to twelve people shared each housing unit with barely enough floor space to accommodate them. Then, all that divided each unit from the next was a thin woven thatch wall, with fifty to seventy people living in each building. In these small, fragile structures, Ly, Kolap, and Thida and all their children lived their lives.

There were flies everywhere, even that close to the beach. We were constantly swatting them away, but they were ever-present in the barracks and relentless around the latrines.

Water for bathing and cleaning came from newly dug open wells, but potable water came in by tanker truck and was distributed in buckets, as was low-grade rice and basic food items like cooking oil and canned items, all overseen by the UN. Meat and vegetables could be purchased from Thai vendors that set up shop across the barbed wire fence. Relief agencies provided donated clothes.

Besides Ly, Kolap, and Thida, there were a number of children about, although it was nearly impossible to figure who was with whom, as the children spilled naturally around the small lot that made up the new Bamboo Camp without much regard to territory or space. As I looked around, Ly tried to introduce me to the others. There was a young, handsome, shirtless man around my age named Sokhy, who Ly introduced as his nephew.

On that first day, after some time with my new friends, I had to rejoin my COERR team. I told them I would return tomorrow. I did not want to leave but knew that I had to make a good impression on my new agency, which had been rather generous in offering me employment.

As I walked back to the COERR building, I looked around the camp. The dense, green jungle mountains leaned down heavily on the flat white strip of sand. Rectangular bamboo barracks with thatch roofing, already turning gray, pointed down like so many icicles. A sea of brown skin, jet-black hair, bright eyes. The unrelenting brightness of the sun. The nearness of the ocean. The barbed wire. The soldiers in bunkers and towers while others patrolled the fences with their automatic rifles. The ocean so close. Unreachable. The mountain so close. Threatening. The mountain concealing the ghosts of those left behind. The past, still close, lingered and leaned down heavily on the flat white strip of sand and the people seeking refuge there.

The Cambodian people, so friendly, so eager to connect with me that I would never be without a crowd around me. As I reached the front gate, one of Thida's daughters, Tevy, came running up to me with a clear plastic bag containing freshly cut pineapple. She shoved it into my hand, smiled, and then disappeared into the crowd.

There was so much to process. But I had to focus. These people needed help. I had to quickly find some way to be useful.

RELIEF WORKER

I settled in to the routine quickly and found little ways to be helpful to the rest of my team, lending a hand here, fetching supplies there, brainstorming and problem-solving in a world that was foreign to all of us expatriates. I immersed myself in this new world, and I felt energized and fulfilled. And for the first time since I had been burned, I felt like I had found a home.

Our team would leave from Trat, where we eventually settled in a rented local home, for the hour-long drive into the camp every morning around seven thirty. My agency, COERR, was assigned to Bamboo Camp where Ly, Kolap, and Thida lived.

The nuns, five Sisters of Mercy from New York, had just arrived and had joined us in camp. Mary, the youngest, was in her thirties. She related to me with ease, and although I had only been in camp for a few days myself, I shared the little I knew, and she was appreciative. The remaining Sisters were all well into their sixties and had never been outside the US. They seemed more than a little shell-shocked by this new world, and they complained about the food, the heat, and the Asian squat toilets. They asked me where my parents were and seemed skeptical of my explanation of how I had come to be with them in the camp. But I quickly appreciated that they were good women who had answered the call when their Order asked for volunteers to help refugees. They would help the Cambodians of Mairut by setting up a sewing center to assist the women with a sustainable vocation, and in time, I would gain their trust and friendship.

The Austrian nurses set up an outpatient clinic in Bamboo Camp under the supervision of a physician from Georgetown University who was stationed at Kamput Camp to the north, but made weekly visits to advise our team. Once the clinic was open, our nurses provided immunizations, preventive exams, and sick call, especially for the children, many of whom had never been seen by nurses or doctors in Cambodia.

French doctors and nurses of Medicine Sans Frontieres (MSF or Doctors Without Borders) ran the camp hospital. They treated malaria, tuberculosis, dengue fever, and dehydration, but also performed emergency surgeries such as appendectomies in a long, thatched, low-roofed bamboo field hospital. They spoke French, wore local clothes, and smoked a lot. Although all were quite fluent in English, they kept to themselves and rarely engaged with the other workers outside the hospital.

Rolf, an eccentric blond German dentist, pulled rotten teeth in a tiny and sparsely appointed bamboo dental clinic. He drove like a maniac in his agency pickup truck, weaving around motorcycles and water buffalo the few times I was daring enough to hitch a ride with him to or from town. Rolf stood out to me because he didn't seem particularly fond of the local people and cultures, but he was awkward with his fellow relief workers as well. I wondered if Rolf had taken refuge here because he hadn't quite fit in at home.

It was an odd crew of expatriates ranging from the highly skilled and experienced doctors and nurses of Medicine Sans Frontiers to people with minimally relevant skills and backgrounds like the nuns—and then there was me. It was slightly organized chaos, and there was no fixed plan. The refugee crisis was still young, and everybody was winging it to some extent.

The UNHCR, with my new Thai friend Dang along with Stephan, the UN field coordinator, oversaw the entire relief operation.

They directed the procurement and distribution of potable water, rice, and other basic foods, coordinated between the various relief agencies, and were our primary interface with Colonel Kosol, the commander for the Thai military in the camp.

Colonel Kosol was the man truly in charge of Mairut Camp. A stern but kind man, he had a reputation as a professional and incorruptible officer. He apparently kept a lid on the kind of exploitation of refugees by Thai vendors that typified the larger camps further north. The barracks for the forty or so soldiers were located just outside the wire of the camp, and the military office was next to the UNHCR office between the old and new camps. Although Kosol was in control, he was diplomatic and worked well with the UNHCR and the aid workers.

I tried to pitch in wherever I saw the opportunity, lending a hand where I could with the setting up of the sewing center, conveying requests for supplies back and forth between the camp and the UNHCR office. I also ran errands directly for the UNHCR team delivering medicines and other supplies to the hospital and clinic in the UNHCR jeep. But I stole away whenever I could to spend time with my new Cambodian friends and learn what I could of the language and culture and recent amazing history of the people.

I could never explain my feelings of the wonder of survival to my friends at home. But here, on the border of Cambodia, I did not have to explain anything. There was a tangible communal sense of having survived. All that mattered for the moment was the present. We had lived to see another day. We had each other. And although the future was uncertain and danger ever present, there was hope in the air.

The Cambodians frequently stared at and asked about my burn scars. Back in the US, out of politeness as defined by American custom, most people avoided commenting on what were obvious scars, but here, it was often the first thing people would ask about, so much so that one of the first Khmer phrases I learned was "*ro liek pleung,*" or "burned by fire."

"In the war?" they inevitably asked.

"No, in an accident in America."

"If you survived such an accident," they said, "then you are favored."

With the basic provisions of food and rudimentary shelter being provided by the UNHCR, international relief organizations, and the Thai, the Cambodians of Mairut Camp could finally relax without worrying where their next meal would come from. The possibility of a better future was coming into focus. For years, they only hoped to survive another day. Now, they began to think about the possibility of a whole new life far from the chaos and horror they left behind them in Cambodia.

"When the American embassy comes here, we hope they will allow us to go live in America," Ly told me. "That will be better. We will be safer. But someday, when peace returns to Cambodia, we will come home again. We are Cambodian and, of course, we would love to return to our country when it is safe."

The residents of "Old Camp" were several years removed from their own narrow escapes, and the hope of a better future had been tempered by years spent languishing behind barbed wire in a small border camp. Despite their violent disenfranchisement during the purges of the Khmer Rouge era and their brutal expulsion, many Old Camp residents still reserved allegiance to the communist mores of the revolution. A thin stretch divided this group of Old Camp refugees who were still loyal to the radical worldview of the overthrown regime from their former victims in the new Bamboo Camp. The residents of Old Camp, mostly rural farmers, were stoic and reserved. The men were much less likely to smile at me, and likely would have had plenty of reason to view an American with suspicion or even contempt. The women were more friendly, but not at all bold or outgoing. They were less interested in going to America, a country they considered to be evil. They had established semi-permanent lives in the camp with well-cultivated gardens surrounding their old and grey wooden barracks.

In the Bamboo Camp, the population was very different. The residents, a mix of Chinese-Khmer and other non-communist Cambodians, were eager to engage with Westerners and even more eager to be rescued from the horrors they had just escaped. They eagerly greeted me as well as any other Western aid worker as we entered the camp.

Still, despite the unsinkable optimism of the Bamboo Camp residents, there were reminders of the recent and inconceivable collective journey of its residents all around. The fragmented families with absent mothers or fathers. The old man with no teeth who had gone crazy and wandered the camp aimlessly talking to ghosts. The building filled with so-called "unaccompanied minors," young children who had been orphaned or separated from their families during the revolution and invasion. The few children among the laughing and happy orphans who would not or could not smile.

The Cambodians were relieved to have escaped their war-torn country, but no one had reached their destination, and safety and security were not guaranteed. I needed to find some way to contribute to the improvement of the refugees, after all, that was why I was there, wasn't it? I had initially been assigned the task of supervising the Khmer refugee workers who would build the new outpatient clinic next to the front gate, but on arriving the first day, the Khmer foreman informed me politely but firmly that they would do just fine without any help from me. They knew how to build a building from bamboo, thank you very much!

Meanwhile, there was a great demand from the residents of the camp to learn English. With Mairut not yet open to foreign embassies, the Thai authorities actively discouraged any formal English teaching program, fearing it might raise hopes of "third country" resettlement when the more likely plan at that point was repatriation—voluntary or forced—back to Cambodia. (In refugee resettlement lingo, the "first country" was the country of origin, the "second country" the country of first refuge, and the "third country" the country of final resettlement—most commonly the US, Canada, France, or Australia). In balancing the demand for learning with the politics of the border, the UNHCR's Stephan Lahusen saw an opportunity. He realized one of my few assets, maybe my only asset, was that I was not taken seriously by the Thai camp command. I was just some kid who hung around with the aid workers. In fact, it was commonly assumed that I was the child of some relief worker. My movements and activities were not scrutinized as closely as the other relief workers or officials and I moved easily among the soldiers who were, after all, roughly my age and found me to be a novelty. And so, it was decided that I would be assigned to surreptitiously teach the teachers English in the school after the normal school day ended.

So, teaching would be my role. Yet, although I didn't fully appreciate it at the time, my most important role would have nothing to do with teaching English. My role was to serve as a witness, and an audience, as a sympathetic ear to the multitude of Cambodian survivors. That role would prove to be the most difficult for me. It was a lot to take in.

The need for people to tell their stories of trauma and survival in the war and under the Khmer Rouge was nearly universal, and people needed to tell their stories to someone from the outside. One by one, people would approach me to tell their stories. Ly, Kolap, and Thida first. Then their neighbors. A few at first. Then more and more.

I had not seen it coming. And it came. Like a tidal wave.

As Ly and I moved around the camp, people would constantly approach us. Other than Ly, almost none spoke English. They spoke Khmer, the new language my brain was just beginning to decode. They spoke in emphatic and urgent tones. Ly calmly, patiently translated every word. And I listened. There was no avoiding it.

Ly was always by my side, my interpreter both in language and in culture, and he treated his fellow Cambodians with great compassion and patience. Ly had a natural and disarming sense of humor. He watched my unfolding amazement as I took my first steps in this new world with appreciation and affection. He also began to patiently teach me Khmer and prompted me to practice and speak it as much as possible. Ly was without his young children, who he had left behind with relatives in Vietnam, and I was far from my family, so we began to form a familial bond as he guided me through a cross-cultural minefield with serenity and grace.

"They want you to tell the outside world about us. They want you to tell the rest of the Americans we are here. Tell the world about the Khmer Rouge, and what they have done. Can you do that?"

"Some of these children," a man name Phaly explained, "saw their own parents killed." Phaly Or was a young man with a wide toothy smile and a mop of hair who oversaw the so-called "unaccompanied minors" section. While it was possible some of the children had merely been separated from their parents, most of them truly were orphans. "This one, this guy," he said, pointing to a quiet dark-skinned boy of nine sitting at a bamboo table drawing in a writing tablet, "he doesn't talk much or smile much, but he drew many pictures of Khmer Rouge soldiers killing the people from his village with machetes, or by tying plastic bags around their heads. The lady from the UNHCR says maybe his parents are still alive somewhere, but I don't think so."

While many of the refugees spoke of family who had been killed, still many more spoke of family members lost to starvation and illness.

"I watched my father get weaker and weaker every day until he could no longer lift his head to drink even a sip of rice broth," one woman recalled. "There was no hospital. There was no medicine. There was no doctor. How could we live like that? How could no one come to help us?"

"I have not seen my family since the evacuation of the Phnom Penh five years ago," a young man told me. "For now, my idea is to go to the US or France or Canada, and then when the war is over, I will go back to Cambodia to find my family."

Ly had a young friend, Kim Sai, who had escaped with his brother. The two were the only survivors of their family.

"My father had been a soldier in the Lon Nol Army. The Khmer Rouge took him out to the field and shot him. Then my mother and my sisters died of starvation. Now, I only have my brother. We cannot go back to Cambodia. Can you help us?"

Very quickly, these painful survival accounts overwhelmed me. It was like hearing Jody Nolan's story of watching his family burn to death over and over again. I felt powerless to ease their pain or offer solutions to the pressing problems of escaping a feared, forced return to war-torn Cambodia. Between the killing and starvation, Cambodia had become a massive grave for too many people. It was impossible for me to absorb it all.

"Will the Thai send us back to Cambodia?" they would ask. "We cannot go back there. We will be killed."

It seemed like everyone wanted something from me because everyone did. I never left camp at the end of the day without a cluster of letters people shoved into my hands with urgent requests to post them in town. While refugees often had little or no money, many had hidden jewelry or gold that they would trade with local Thai merchants who would sell basic goods and meat and vegetables along the fence. Others had money sent by friends or relatives in the US or Canada. Still, while my interactions with the Cambodians had that transactional quality born of circumstance, I did feel that mostly they needed to be noticed. To be acknowledged. They needed their stories to be heard.

Having never cared about current events or news before, I found myself starved for information from any outside source that might provide a context for the situation I found on the border. I didn't get it. I was so ill-prepared. While I certainly knew there had been a war in Vietnam, I didn't understand this Cambodian piece. How did the war spread to Cambodia? Why did the US bomb the country? Where did the Khmer Rouge come from? Oh the irony—for the first time in my life I saw the relevance of news and information, and I was cut off from the outside world in a small remote refugee camp.

In town, we would get one-day-old copies of the *Bangkok Post*, Thailand's largest English language newspaper. Our team passed around well-worn copies of Francoise Ponchaud's *Cambodia Year Zero*, one of the first accounts of the brutal Khmer Rouge regime, and we learned of the American entanglement in this story through William Shawcross's *Sideshow*. I devoured these books.

In reading *Sideshow* and *Year Zero*, I came to understand how the US expanded the Vietnam War into technically neutral Cambodia to flush out and destroy the so-called "Ho Chi Minh Trail" used by North Vietnamese to supply communist guerillas in South Vietnam.

When the initial US invasion proved wildly unpopular in the US, the strategy switched to a massive carpet bombing across Cambodia and supported the overthrow of Prince Sihanouk in favor of US allied General Lon Nol. The bombing drove resentment of the US-backed Lon Nol regime, and gave momentum to the Cambodian communist movement, the Khmer Rouge. When the Khmer Rouge overthrew the Lon Nol government in April 1975 and the Americans evacuated, they emptied the cities and began a purge of all Western influences in an effort to restore Cambodia to its historic twelfth-century agrarian glory. The effort was a disaster, and famine followed. Efforts to identify and eliminate people perceived to be contaminated by the west and intraparty purges led to the execution of thousands. Starvation took the lives of thousands more. It was believed between one and two million out of a total of seven and a half million Cambodians perished under the Khmer Rouge.

In 1979, the Vietnamese invaded Cambodia and overthrew the Khmer Rouge and installed a new government. The remnants of the Khmer Rouge, along with people trying to escape the Khmer Rouge, all amassed on the Thai-Cambodian border. And there we were.

There we were—for the moment. While there was palpable relief among the refugees for having survived the war, starvation, and killing in Cambodia, the Cambodians on the border remained on the razor's edge. At any moment, they could be pushed back into the pit of hell. The threat of forced repatriation to war-torn Vietnamese-occupied Cambodia hung in the air. Even the Khmer Rouge who had tormented the residents of the Bamboo Camp were just a stone's throw away in the Old Camp of Mairut.

In the camps, there were a few precious, cheaply manufactured shortwave radios. We crowded around them with their whistling and drifting signals, catching parts of BBC and Voice of America (VOA) broadcasts that occasionally would include a brief fragment of a news item relating to fighting along the border or the status of the international relief operation both on the border and inside Cambodia.

One day as we listened to a VOA broadcast in Ly's barracks, the rather stiff and formal announcer declared that it was time for a sample of "American Popular Music of Today." Across the crackling speaker, I heard the strains of Tom Petty's "Refugee," then a big hit back home. It immediately brought me home. As the song played on, the vocal refrain "You don't—have—to live like a refugee" raised the eyebrows of Ly's friend, Kim Sai. At first, he looked perplexed. Then he was angry.

"What does he mean, I don't have to live like a refugee? What choice do I have? Doesn't he understand that the refugee does not have a choice?"

I did my best to explain that Tom Petty indeed had no idea what it was like to be a refugee, and that he was speaking metaphorically, a concept I had difficulty making clear with my lack of Khmer skills and the rudimentary English command of Kim Sai. It struck me that as American teenagers kicked back with this song, likely few of them even gave passing thought to the plight of the displaced and dispossessed on the Cambodian border, and, as Kim Sai had so emphatically stated, their lack of choice concerning their position.

Was the world aware of these people? Would they be saved? As I contemplated their situation, I couldn't help feeling despondent. No one had understood anything about the Shriners back in my hometown. And no one else seemed to notice or care when I showed them the stories about the Cambodians before I left. Why would they care now?

But I could not let on. Not to my new friends who, after all, I was supposed to be helping.

LY AND KOLAP

Ly was my cultural guide and interpreter and I depended on him. In our earliest conversations, he asked how I came to be in Mairut. Had I come with my parents? By myself? Why? I told him about the news coverage about the Cambodian refugees in the US. I even told him about my burns, how I saw things differently. I told him I couldn't look away. He seemed completely satisfied with my answers.

Like other Cambodians, Ly had not hesitated to ask about my burns. He had lost a finger in a lumber mill accident, but he was philosophical about it. "We are still here, you and I."

He had much to teach me about Cambodia and recent events. Fortunately for me, both of us had nothing but time.

Ly explained that he had been orphaned as a child and had been raised by a Vietnamese woman who had been a neighbor of his parents, street vendors who died when he was too young to even remember them.

"You know, in the twelfth century, Cambodia controlled much of Southeast Asia, including what is now Vietnam, Laos, and Thailand. And during this time, Cambodia built the great Angkor Wat temple in Siem Riep province." Ly was clearly proud of his heritage.

"When peace returns to Cambodia, I will return to my country. And you will come to Cambodia and Kolap and I will greet you there.

"Cambodia was a happy and peaceful place when I was young. But, you know, then the war came, and it was very bad. I was living in Phnom Penh, and I used to hang around with the foreign journalists to practice my English. Things were easier under Sihanouk's time until 1970, but when Lon Nol came to power, the war, the fighting, expanded. The Lon Nol government was corrupt. And then the Americans bombed the country too, and the Khmer Rouge began to grow in their power.

"In 1975, the Khmer Rouge took over, and things were very bad. They emptied Phnom Penh overnight. They moved everyone to the countryside. They killed everyone who had been in the Lon Nol government, and they killed educated people and other people they did not like or people who had worked with the Americans. They hated people with Chinese blood. Everyone was forced to work in the fields, building irrigation ditches and farming.

"They took all the clothes and made everyone wear the black pajamas and rubber sandals made from old tires."

Having relocated the population to the countryside, the Khmer Rouge attempted to reproduce the ancient glory of the Angkor period, when sophisticated irrigation systems allowed multiple crops of rice per year. As the modern era had only brought decline to Cambodia, the Khmer Rouge romanticized the Angkor history, and aimed for a return to a simple agrarian society, this time on a communist foundation.

In the early chaos of the Khmer Rouge advance on Phnom Penh, Ly was able to buy his way onto a fleeing army helicopter bound for the port of Kompong Som. From there, he made his way by boat to Vietnam where he would live as a refugee. Within two weeks of his arrival, Saigon fell to the North Vietnamese, and Ly found himself a refugee from a communist regime in a second newly communist country. He survived by cunning and instinct, living without documentation on the fringes of the war-torn former capital of now vanquished South Vietnam.

About a year after arriving, he met Kolap. She had recently fled Cambodia to Vietnam with her children after they'd survived a year as slave laborers in a Khmer Rouge evacuation village. Kolap was of mixed race, including Chinese and Laotian lineage. She and her family had been evacuated from Phnom Penh when the Khmer Rouge came to power. She was labeled as "new people," the term used for people evacuated from the cities who were to be reeducated to the worthy life of rural peasants. When she saw increasing persecution of non-ethnic Khmer evacuees in her new village, she and her young family undertook a risky escape under cover of night. Miraculously, they made it to Vietnam without being captured.

By the time they met, Kolap had separated from her husband. Ly and Kolap fell in love (almost instantly, Ly would say) and Ly took her young children as his own. Together, they lived an unsettled life on the fringes in Ho Chi Minh City, the former Saigon, buying and selling things like cigarettes, liquor, and antibiotics on the black market.

In 1979, the Vietnamese invaded Cambodia to overthrow the Khmer Rouge. Ly and Kolap believed that this was their opportunity to try to make it to Thailand where they could escape to the west—Canada or the United States. But the journey across Vietnamese-occupied Cambodia and over a heavily mined border was not one for children. So, they made the difficult decision to leave their three young children with relatives and undertake the journey with only their nephew, Chan Sokhy. Once they reached freedom, they would make an application through international agencies to have their minor children reunited with them in a free country.

That was the plan. The trek across Cambodia from southern Vietnam was difficult, especially as they only had flip-flops on their feet and very little gold to barter with. They found the Thai border impassable at first.

While gathered with other refugees near the border, they first heard about the incident at Preah Vihear.

In June 1979, shortly before Ly and Kolap arrived in Thailand, the Thai military forcibly repatriated between thirty to forty thousand

Cambodian refugees back into Cambodia at gunpoint. The refugees had gathered in three camps north of the town of Aranyaprathet on the border, but the Thai did not recognize them as refugees and wanted to discourage others from trying to cross into Thailand. The soldiers gathered the Cambodians on buses, explaining that they were being moved to another camp. Most of the refugees were women, children, and the elderly, and many were in poor health and malnourished. They were driven far north on the border and then forced down steep mountain trails—survivors described it as a cliff—back into Cambodia. The trails were heavily mined, and it was rumored that thousands had perished on the forced journey.

Ly and Kolap were discouraged by the news of the repatriation. Still, having come so far, they were determined to make it to freedom so they could send for their children.

And so, several months before I met them, they had managed to cross the border at night, carefully following footstep by footstep those who had walked ahead of them to avoid unexploded land mines. Upon entering Thai territory, they were immediately discovered by Thai soldiers and arrested and placed in a small border jail.

"That is where we met Thida. She and her children were the only other family held in the jail. We felt sorry for her, a mother with so many children and her husband dead from the Khmer Rouge. We befriended her, and we have stayed with her ever since."

Together, they were brought to Sakeo Camp, a new camp formed inside of Thai territory in response to a large influx of starving refugees. This was in late October 1979, and the pictures of the starving refugees in that camp were the ones that first caught my eye in news reports back home in the states.

Ly was among the healthier refugees at Sakeo, and with his English skills, was recruited to assist the voluntary agencies working to help the starving refugees. He worked as an interpreter for World Vision and later helped both Australian and Canadian embassy delegations. He hoped that his good work there would lead to an offer for resettlement in a "third country."

"Sakeo was very bad. So many people were starving, and many

people died there. Also, so many of the people there were Khmer Rouge. We were very uncomfortable being there, so when they asked for people to be moved to Mairut, we volunteered."

They had arrived in Mairut only a few weeks before my arrival. While they felt better in Mairut (at least the Khmer Rouge refugees were separated into a different camp), they now realized that they were still stuck, confined inside barbed wire patrolled by armed soldiers, just like Sakeo. And always rumors about another forced repatriation like Preah Vihear. And the camp was not open to embassies for resettlement processing. In fact, at that time, none of the border camps were. The Thai were determined to discourage further refugee flow into Thailand, and they figured resettlement offers would do the opposite.

"Kolap gets headaches every day. She is worried about her children in Vietnam. She is worried she may never see them again. I am worried too, but we will try to do everything to get to the third country so we can reunite with them.

"Please, Scott. Help us get to a third country, the US, Canada, or Australia. It is the only way we can get our children. You must help us."

Here we were. Ly and Kolap had left their children behind in Vietnam and did not know when they would see them again. There was no way to communicate with them except through very slow and unreliable mail. I had left my family behind for very different reasons. I had no way to communicate with them—except through slow and unreliable mail. We were all separated from our families. Ly and Kolap were worried sick about their children. My parents must have been worried about me, and I felt guilty about that. But I was here now, and I had to focus on helping the people I came to help.

Ly was a survivor. He was adept, highly intelligent, and personable. He had excellent command of English. He had hung out with Western journalists in Phnom Penh before the fall; he had skillfully negotiated with Thai soldiers and refugee workers and had aided relief workers and embassy workers alike. Kolap also was a survivor and had supported herself as a single mother living in exile in

Vietnam before she met Ly. She was also wise beyond her years, almost mystical in her observations and insights. Ly confessed that he always took her advice without question. Whenever she said it was time to move, he moved. While the odds were often against them, they were a formidable duo.

In contrast, Thida was vulnerable. She could not speak English. While she had already demonstrated the will to survive and gave off a sense of spiritual inner strength, she was an unaccompanied woman in a male dominated military zone. She was saddled with seven young children and had no real prospects for resettlement or self-support. From the start, I worried about her the most.

15
THIDA

Through Ly, I was able to converse with Thida and learn her story.
Thida had led a quiet but comfortable life before the war. In 1962, an attractive and personable teenager, she met and fell in love with a young middle school arts teacher. They were soon married and not long after, they moved to Battambang in western Cambodia to begin their new life together.

Thida's husband was a gifted man who taught traditional Khmer music and dance in the schools of Battambang, a rural province bordering Thailand. His talents and industriousness won him promotions and advancements, and he ultimately became a provincial director of the public school fine arts programs for the entire province.

Over the next dozen years, the family grew—by the end of the Lon Nol period, Thida and her husband had seven children together. They prospered in a peaceful setting and were treated with respect by the members of their local community. Thida's husband was often invited to dine with the governor of Battambang, and when outdoor movie shows would come to town, the family was given VIP seats in the front row.

But their idyllic life of modest privilege would not last. With the American bombing and the rise of communist insurgents, the country disintegrated into war. In April 1976, the communist Khmer Rouge overthrew the Lon Nol government. When the revolutionary regime came to Battambang, Thida's husband's education and affiliation with the deposed regime suddenly became a liability.

Young Khmer Rouge soldiers abruptly took control of their village. Thida's husband's education and government job marked him as an enemy of the revolution. He and his family were forced to relocate to a "new village." As "new people," they were marked for harsh treatment.

The "new village" was about a day's walk from their old home. In the new village, Thida, her family, and other evacuees were given black pajamas and rubber tire sandals, the somber uniform of the revolution. The newly relocated Cambodians of the new village were subjected to long and tedious indoctrination lectures about the corruption of their former lives. Thida and her husband were sent to the fields from dawn to dusk to do manual labor digging irrigation ditches. Food rations were meager.

"It was very difficult, Scott," Thida said through Ly. "We lost everything. We lost our home. We lost our money. We lost our freedom."

This was the only time I saw Thida subdued or sad. When she told her own story, her trademark smile vanished, and her voice became soft and flat.

Eventually, the older children were sent away to live and work in "mobile youth teams." Once separated on the youth teams, the older children were rarely permitted to return home to visit their family. Kanya, the eldest daughter, became sickly early on and was allowed to return to her family. But Chanthy and Tevy, her second and third daughters, then in their early teens, spent much of the nearly four years under the Khmer Rouge away in separate youth camps (Chanthy in the *Kong Chalat* for older teens, Tevy in the *Kong Komar* for the younger teens), overseen and abused by armed teenage Khmer Rouge soldiers. The teenagers were put to work every day for long hours digging irrigation ditches, clearing jungle, and planting pumpkins and other vegetables. The little food that was produced was rationed for them, so what little free time they had was spent supplementing their diet by foraging for wild mushrooms, roots, and whatever they could grow for themselves in hidden gardens.

Thida and her husband continued to labor ten- and twelve-hour days in the rice fields with scant food rations under the unsympathetic direction of the young Khmer Rouge cadre. Eventually, the effort to turn back the clock to the agrarian past failed to produce an adequate harvest, and famine swept across the countryside. While many high-ranking members of the former regime had been taken away and executed in killing fields, even more would die of starvation.

After nearly four years of suffering slave labor and abuse, Thida's husband became ill with a pox virus that spread through the village. He had been a teacher, not a farmer, and he was a thin man when the Khmer Rouge had first come to power. He was much thinner now. Malnourished, he grew weaker. And then he died.

Thida and Kanya and the younger children were with him when he died at the age of forty-four. Chanthy was allowed to return to see her father and arrived only moments before he passed. Then she was sent back to her work camp. There was no funeral. The body of Thida's husband was placed on a cart and taken away.

Thida, barely thirty-two years old, found herself alone with seven minor children, the eldest a mere sixteen and the youngest just three. "*P'dey kyum slap aw hay.*" My husband died—a phrase I learned quickly in Khmer because I would hear it repeated so often from so many refugees in the camps.

Thida's husband had died a mere two months before her village was liberated by the Vietnamese army who had invaded Cambodia to depose the Khmer Rouge. After the Vietnamese invasion, Thida gathered up her children and tried to return to her pre-revolution home, but found it occupied. She subsequently settled in a neighboring village and took up work buying rice and other basic items at the border and carrying them back to the village to resell at a modest profit.

Under the Vietnamese, she never felt safe, and she saw no real future for her children. One night, she pulled all seven together and made the perilous journey through the minefields to the border with Thailand. When she arrived at the border, she was immediately apprehended by the Thai border guards who threatened to shoot her if she did not return to Cambodia.

"Then shoot me," she said. "We are not going back."

The Thai soldier yielded, and she and the children were taken to the border jail. That is where she met Ly and Kolap.

She did not know what she would do now. She only knew she could not go back to Cambodia. "If I go back," she said, "they will kill me." Many Cambodian refugees feared death on return to Cambodia. They had already seen too many people die. The threat was real. The best available official estimates published in the international press set the death toll from the Khmer Rouge regime as high as two million, roughly a third of the country's prewar population. While the Vietnamese forces had toppled the Khmer Rouge regime in Phnom Penh, the remnants of the Khmer Rouge were still armed and active along the Thai-Cambodian border. The fear of death on return to Cambodia hung over the border camps like a dense cloud.

Thida and her children, along with Ly and Kolap, were first moved to Sakeo Camp in Thailand, the camp where they were surrounded by the starving and sickly remnants of the Khmer Rouge who were fleeing the Vietnamese forces. When an opportunity arose, they volunteered to be moved to the new camp at Mairut, where, within days of their arrival, fate would bring us together.

In Mairut Camp, I also go to know Thida's children, all seven of them. The eldest daughter was Kanya. She was my age. In my first days in Building 19, Kanya was ever present and always silent. She was painfully shy; she always managed to be as far away from me as possible in such a crowded space. She was a petite, malnourished young woman with a soft complexion and mournful eyes that betrayed a heavy heart despite her efforts to reveal as little of herself as possible. Her brown, shoulder-length hair would fall around her neck and face as she looked down, as she often did in my presence. She moved about the barracks without a sound and almost without notice, like a ghost, crouching to wash a dish, slipping behind us to tend to a younger sibling, quietly studying in an English primer. She rarely, if ever, left the small living space of her temporary home in Building 19. When I learned she and I were nearly the same age, I was immediately interested in knowing her better, but her habit of looking down in my presence and her tendency to maximize the distance between us made it clear that it would not be possible any time soon. There was something about Kanya that set her apart from the other children. They were all resilient given their circumstances, but I sensed that somehow, she was more deeply traumatized than the others. I almost never saw her smile or laugh. The opposite of her mother.

For that very reason, I suppose, Kanya presented a challenge. But I was eager to gain her trust. I wanted to know her. I tried to talk to her. I tried to joke with her. She always turned or even ran away. Rarely would I get her to smile. A brief smile, a blush. But her silent response to my efforts said in no uncertain terms, "please just leave me alone!"

Chanthy, the second daughter, was sixteen. Taller than her elder sister and often mistakenly assumed to be the eldest, she had thick, wavy black hair, bright eyes, and a wide smile. She likely had suffered as much as Kanya in the preceding years, but she was much more self-assured and quicker to laugh. I was able to make a tenuous connection with her through a very cheap, untunable guitar that was floating around the camp, and my rendition of the Herman's Hermits' "Leaning on a Lamp Post" made her laugh out loud. She was modest, like Kanya, but not as shy. She had some of her mother's boldness and would often venture out into the camp with a girlfriend or two. She was the first to try speaking English words in front of me. She was willing to laugh at her own errors but was nonetheless a very eager and self-disciplined student.

The next daughter, Tevy, who had run after me with the pineapple on my first day, was fourteen. She was quite small for her age, perhaps a result of malnutrition during adolescence. She always had an endearing smile. With her wavy hair and perfectly angled facial features, her face resembled the classic faces on the temple of Bayon that I had seen in old copies of the *National Geographic*. She seemed oblivious to the worries and cares that burdened her mother and older sisters, a happy product of her youth.

Next were the three boys, Vongsa, Rasmey, and Komar, then thirteen, eleven, and ten respectively. They, like any boys their age, made the best of the open community of the camp, running freely between the bamboo barracks among their little friends. Komar was the one most inclined to stay closer to home, and he was more than happy to climb all over me. Rasmey was the little man, with a confident walk and a broad smile. Vongsa, it seems, was almost always somewhere else, but when he was around, he displayed the easygoing personality that typified the family.

Malis, the four-year-old, was the youngest. She clung to her mother, and her mother clung to her. If Thida was wounded, Malis was her medicine.

Malis's arms and legs bore the marks of impetigo, a skin infection common among the children in the camps that caused redness, crusting, and faint scars. These wounds did not dampen her spirit, though, and it was a delight to watch her thrive in the warm glow of her mother's love.

Thida's three eldest daughters were all young women who cooked, cleaned, and watched the younger children, a great help to Thida. But Malis, Thida's youngest daughter, was her baby. She was always underfoot, or holding on to Thida's leg, or crawling over her. Thida was a taskmaster over her older children, often issuing short direct orders and rebukes to keep them well behaved and on top of their domestic chores, but she treated Malis differently. Holding Malis close as she relaxed in the midday heat appeared to have a soothing effect on Thida.

One day I brought some toys I had purchased in Trat to give to the younger children. They had nothing, and I wanted them to have something of their own. They were pleased and gracious in receiving them. They played with them and shared them with their little friends. Then those toys made their way around the entire camp. The children had no notion of ownership of a material object, and they had every notion of communal living, which is all they had ever known.

To the young children, the refugee camp was not such a terrible place. They were happy and free to play among themselves. This was the striking divide between the youngest children and those old enough to know and remember the despotic regime they had narrowly escaped, old enough to fear the uncertain future and the possibility of a forced return to their ravaged country.

In those early days, Ly, Kolap, Thida, and I savored the gift of a new friendship. It was an intense time in both their lives and mine. None of us knew where we were going or what would happen next. Big things were happening. There was great opportunity. There was great danger. It all was overpowering.

I believe they found my friendship an unexpected and welcome tie to the outside world. I found their friendship the only way I could relate to and comprehend the unbearable volume of loss and suffering that was pouring over me, survival story by survival story.

For such an uncertain and precarious time, as we all knew it to be, we laughed often. They had all just survived the killing fields. We celebrated the moment by singing and listening to cassette tapes of Western music that had been popular in Cambodia before the war. To my delight, they loved the Beatles as much as I did. They also loved Creedence Clearwater Revival and Santana. They always asked me to sing "Let It Be" as I strummed the precious, barely tunable guitar that was floating about the camp.

"Do you know how to play the Bee Gees "I Started a Joke"?" Ly asked.

That was a song in my small repertoire that I already knew. To their delight, I sang it, and they requested it again and again. It was a song about a joke that made the world cry.

There was a certain inner calm I found when I was in the company of Ly, Kolap, and Thida. It is not as if I had starved for love back home, for my own family was very nurturing and supportive. My parents, family, and friends had certainly tried very hard to understand me, but I felt like they couldn't relate to what I had been through, what I had come to know, and most of all, they could not help me understand how I was supposed to move forward in a world where everyone seemed not to notice or acknowledge the suffering of others.

If there was anyone who understood suffering, it was the Cambodians.

In the company of my new friends, and in the odd setting of the seemingly unlikely and precarious peace of a camp where the silence expanded to fill the space between the often violent and explosive events of the border, I felt an easing of the turmoil deep inside me, a turmoil I knew so well but understood so little.

One of the things that impressed me most was how the Cambodians who had been separated from family or who had lost family by murder or starvation cobbled and pieced together new families from the remnants of the old family and new and chance relationships made in the camps. Although in Asia it is customary to refer to close friends and neighbors with terms denoting familial ties, such as brother Khy, or Aunt Thyrann, this was different. Fragments of families adopted fragments of other families and formed new family units that functioned as traditional families.

In this manner, Ly and Kolap, separated from their children, had adopted Thida and her children, who had lost their husband and father. Ly's nephew, Sokhy, was adopted as a brother. And a single unaccompanied woman, with no obvious near relations of her own, was invited into the fold as a cousin until a later time when she was reunited with survivors from her original family.

Therefore, it was without forethought or plan that I was simply and naturally added into the mix. Kolap, who had already taken a maternal role in my life, had me address her as "*Madai*," which means mother. The children were "*B'u-on*," or younger siblings. Of course, this was a somewhat artificial construction, at least to a Westerner. I had not replaced Ly and Kolap's actual children, whom they missed terribly, any more than they replaced my actual parents. But, in their eyes, and in a way, I would learn and come to accept as perfectly natural the idea that I would be an additional son and that they would be additional parents; and it occurred without much discussion at all.

One day, early in this process, I asked Ly how I should address Thida. Should I call her "*Madai*," too, or maybe "*Ming*," which means aunt?

Ly looked at me with a serious face. "You should call Thida '*Madai k'mae kyum Thida*.'" He practiced the pronunciation with me until I had it right.

Shortly, Thida herself returned to the barracks. Ly nodded at me.

"*Chum Riep Sua, Madai k'mae kyum Thida*," I said, greeting Thida in my clearest Khmer.

Thida looked shocked, then laughed. Ly had fallen to his side, curled over in deep convulsions of laughter. Their laughter was accompanied by squeals and howls from everyone in the vicinity of Building 19 who had heard my greeting.

Ly then brought me in on the joke. I had just said, "Greetings, my mother-in-law Thida."

Well, that joke proved too funny for everyone, and from that point on, Thida was referred to as "*madai k'mae*" and I was adopted as the son-in-law. It occurred to me briefly and in passing that this way of addressing Thida might cause some concern to Kanya and Chanthy who may have wondered if there was something more to it. But it was a joke. It was their joke, so I played along.

We all needed a good laugh.

16

THIDA'S TOUCH

The unlikely bond that had begun when Thida boldly grabbed my hand that first day continued to grow. Thida had connected with me so directly and unexpectedly—by touch. As time went on, she was still the only Cambodian I knew to claim a sort of physical intimacy with me. I had little experience with that kind of interaction, and even less with someone so nonchalantly reaching out and holding my disfigured right hand. So easily. As if there was nothing wrong with me.

She chose to sit close to me, to tap me on the wrist or to nudge my shoulder as she teased me. At first, when she held my hand, I was alarmed. But soon I found I liked being close to her. In a harsh and threatening world, where the constant pleas and supplications of the refugees quickly enveloped and overwhelmed me, she seemed to shield me from the onslaught of the crowd with her singular warmth and charm.

I was unable to resist her. I was far from home. I had just arrived in a foreign land—in a refugee camp. I felt pressure to perform as an adult, pressure to respond to the endless appeals for my help, pressure to stand strong and not fall apart. And if I couldn't do it, I would have to fake it. But here, in the middle of all this harsh reality, in this surreal new world where I was completely over my head, was Thida. Even when she wasn't smiling or laughing, her face was serene, almost ethereal. I wouldn't have been able to explain it to someone; it was a feeling I couldn't even explain to myself. But somehow, she calmed me. When I was close to her, the dark sense of impending doom I'd carried ever since the burn ward faded away.

Why did I focus my concern and attention on her above all others? Thida was physically attractive, vulnerable as a widow with seven minor children, and in a most desperate situation. She had little control or power over her fate. I was seventeen, looking for someone to help. I wanted to be needed, and she needed to be helped. But mostly, I focused on her because of the way I felt when I was near her. I hadn't felt this calm since surviving the fire.

What did Thida see in me? I'm not sure. Sure, she needed a friend like me. An American. A person who could advocate for her, who could help her escape. Yet somehow, I felt that she genuinely *liked* me too. As time went on, I became confident that her affection was real. It showed in how comfortable she was with me, in her physical warmth and in her humor.

One day, quite early on, she reached over and gently slapped my belly.

"What was that for?" I asked.

"*Scott towat na!*—Scott is fat!"

Everyone laughed. At five feet eight inches, I weighed 120 pounds wet. But among the survivors of famine and starvation under the Khmer Rouge, I was fat. I laughed too, happy to serve as the butt of a Thida joke.

Thida would constantly tease me in Khmer, and when the others laughed, I would look to Ly to translate the joke. Then we'd all laugh together.

My eagerness to make Thida laugh too motivated my earliest efforts to learn the Khmer language. Ly was happy to help me master just enough vocabulary to say something silly. For example, when I would try to get her to study her English, she would dismiss me saying "*Thida k'jil rien.*" Thida is too lazy to learn. So, in response, when she would try to teach me a new Khmer word or phrase, I would wrap my lips over my teeth to mimic toothlessness and then I'd say *"K'yum jah hay, bat t'main hay, plait aw hay, rien mun baan te."* I'm old, I've lost my teeth, I've forgotten everything, I can't learn. With limited material, I repeated those lines often. But the act never failed to tickle my new friends.

How could Thida laugh so easily in her circumstances? How could she be so happy, so serene, after everything she had been through? She was stuck in a bamboo refugee camp surrounded by barbed wire and landmines, only yards away from the Khmer Rouge camp, and well within Vietnamese artillery range—and yet she found joy in every day. She was giving of herself to those around her when I might have believed she had nothing left to give.

Thida wanted to know about my parents. She wanted to know why I was not in school. Where did I sleep when I wasn't in camp? Who cooked my food? Who washed my clothes? Through Ly, she peppered me with questions. No one else did that. And then, often, she would ask if I could help her. Was there any chance she could come to the United States and live with me?

I was a kid working as a volunteer for an agency. I never had more than twenty dollars in my pocket. I had little or nothing concrete to help her with. But to her, I had everything. I could walk outside the gate. So desperate was her situation, a destitute American teenager represented her best shot at getting out of a border refugee camp to freedom.

Although I had very little money, I bought simple items for my new friends from the market in Trat. Early on, after seeing Kolap and Thida wearing the same clothes every day, I purchased two new sarongs for each of them when I went to town. Later that same day, I was startled when Thida placed her hands on my back and shoulders as I sat talking with Ly. I turned to see what she wanted, but she just laughed and turned and spoke to Kolap.

The next morning when I arrived in camp, Thida and Kolap presented me with a shirt they had sewn for me by hand—made from one of the sarongs I had given them. Thida had placed her hands on my shoulders to measure my size. The shirt fit me like a glove.

"Every day, Scott wears the same T-shirt," Thida explained through Ly. "Even the refugees have more clothes than he does!"

Thida had successfully survived the Khmer Rouge regime, the Vietnamese occupation, and had crossed a mine-filled border with seven children. While she remained at risk as a woman with small children on the border, she knew how to survive. Out of thousands of refugees, she was the one who had successfully secured my attention. As a young man still learning my way, I watched her closely. I immediately sensed that she had much to teach me about how to live in a world with so much pain and suffering. She had been through so much, but she still seemed to find moments of lightness and hope in a sea of utter despair.

Why had I left my home and traveled so far? What was I looking for?

Maybe it was Thida I had been looking for.

She helped me simply by existing, by being Thida, by showing me tenderness, by smiling, laughing, and loving in the aftermath of utter horror. She believed in me and never doubted me. Her faith in me helped me believe I could go forward with hope, with laughter, with human connection. And through her I was beginning to learn how to channel the compassion I felt for the suffering of others in a meaningful way, how to give of myself even if I felt I had so little to give. She was modeling for me how to seize the moment, to take risks, to join together with people, to make new friends, to take a chance at trusting people you just met. New friends who I could relate to in ways I could not connect with my peers back home; people who had been through the depths of agony yet emerged on the other side. And she was teaching me that I could still smile, love, laugh, and still find joy in a harsh and unforgiving world. Not only could I do it, I *had* to do it. This was the only way forward.

Her optimism seemed irreconcilable with her situation. Unlike the masculine role models for surviving I had met before, she represented something entirely different and beguiling. Survival untethered to gloom. Survival with room for joy.

There was something about Thida that drew me to her almost

immediately. How does one account for attraction? Her smile and laughter were infectious. She brightened the dark place we were in. The fact that she, almost uniquely among the overwhelming numbers of survivors in the camp, showed me affection, both emotionally and physically, combined with strength and optimism, made her singular among a sea of survivors. Whatever it was, I was attracted to her by the same overpowering force that had brought me to Thailand. In no time at all, we connected.

Ly and Kolap were role models in survival as well, and Ly was truly my cultural guide on my day-by-day journey to learn about the Cambodian people and their culture. They genuinely cared for me, and they too knew how to extract meaning and joy out of every moment. But there was something special about Thida that gave me hope and made me feel happy for the first time in years.

REFUGEE LIMBO

Although everyone in the Bamboo Camp was relieved to have made it to the relative safety of Thai territory, the goal was clear: resettlement in a "third country." The US was by far the third country of preference. For Ly and Kolap, the goal had greater urgency than most, because it was a necessary step in order for them to be reunified with their young children. At the time of my arrival, no embassies had been authorized by the Thai authorities to have contact with the residents of Mairut. The Thai government still had reservations about the potential for embassy presence to attract even greater numbers of refugees to cross into Thailand.

Ly, Kolap, and Thida wasted no time in enlisting my assistance in pursuing the goal of resettlement, and I was more than happy to do what little I could. We worked with the folklore and misinformation about the resettlement process that flourished in the complete absence of embassy resettlement programs in Mairut Camp. On my brief visits to Bangkok, I visited the Canadian and Australian embassies on Ly's behalf, as he had written to them asking for asylum after helping translate for their delegations in Sakeo. The embassy staffers were polite to me but could make no firm commitments. There is a process, they said.

Some refugees in camp who had relatives in the US had received sponsorship papers, loosely binding notarized signed documents executed in the United States under the auspices of a voluntary agency working in the refugee resettlement effort on the state side. Those with sponsorship papers seemed to be the most likely to have their correspondence answered, and the rumor quickly spread that the sponsorship forms were prerequisite documents required to gain the attention of the embassy.

I wanted so much to help, but alone I had no standing. But I thought perhaps I could ask my parents. I immediately wrote them asking if they would be willing to file sponsorship papers for Ly's and Thida's families: Dear Mom and Dad, I know I just ran away from home, but I need you to assume responsibility for ten people I just met, only one of whom can speak English. I need you to do this and quickly.

There was some back and forth and they naturally asked many questions. In the end, even though they remained quite apprehensive about what they were getting into, my parents came through. Two months after my arrival in Thailand, a turn of events they had neither anticipated nor planned, my mother and father filed sponsorship papers to accept responsibility for both families through the Hartford chapter of the United States Catholic Conference, the designated resettlement agency for all of Connecticut.

When we finally received photocopies of the sponsorship papers for Ly and Kolap and Thida's entire family, there was celebration and a sense of relief.

Unfortunately, the importance of these types of sponsorships in securing resettlement in the US was greatly overestimated in the camps. At the time, none of us understood that the process was much more complicated. First, the UNHCR, with the blessing of the Thai Ministry of the Interior, would have to open the camps to foreign embassies for resettlement processing. Then, the "third countries" of the US, Canada, France, and Australia, among others, would have to process applications. All countries had ranking that prioritized connections to the resettlement country. Generally, the highest priority was placed on those who had worked with or served the third-country government (such as former embassy staff) or supported their allies (in the case of Cambodia, the Lon Nol regime). Next in priority were those with first-degree relatives in the third country. After that, priority was placed on refugees least likely to become a burden on the third-country governments, including individuals with skills and education, uncommon qualities among the rural survivors of the Khmer Rouge (many of the educated elite of Cambodia had not survived the Khmer Rouge). Finally, all other things being equal, those with sponsors were seen as more desirable. Sponsors were individuals in the third country who had formally taken on responsibility through volunteer resettlement agencies to provide support for the refugees after their arrival in the new country. Once ranked, a lucky minority of refugees would be called for interviews for the chance for resettlement.

At this point, no embassies had even been allowed to enter the Cambodian camps to process refugees in any significant numbers. The Thai were worried that offering third-country resettlement would merely draw more refugees to the border from inside Cambodia, so they closed off the border camps to foreign embassies except for the most compelling cases. For the time being, there would be no large-scale processing of refugees on the Cambodian border.

Ly and Kolap had no relatives in "third countries," and having relatives, especially first-degree relatives, in Canada, France, or the US was the best chance for a ticket out. Thida had no known relations outside of Cambodia.

Although neither Ly's or Thida's family had an obvious claim, and therefore were both not likely to be called by an embassy even if the embassies were ever allowed access to this camp, Ly had used every opportunity to capitalize on making contacts and enlisting advocates. I was obviously one of them. Prior to meeting me, Ly had interpreted for doctors of the World Vision program. He had also interpreted for the Canadian embassy. Although his service had been brief, it at least created a possible claim of service to an embassy. In any case, anyone who had met Ly could not help but be impressed with his intelligence and charm. From an employment and self-sufficiency angle, he was a good bet. A few of his previous agency allies were already working behind the scenes on his behalf, and I was doing what I could.

Thida's family was the challenge. With no obvious claim for resettlement anywhere, and no contacts other than myself, she was in great danger of getting lost in the chaos and shuffle of the border. In addition, she lacked the language skills, and in terms of level of anticipated care and support, a young widow with seven minor children was not an attractive prospect from the viewpoint of any country's immigration program. Every time I saw Thida, every time I thought of her, I fretted about how best to secure her safety. Other than filing sponsorship papers, I had no idea where to begin, but I was determined to get Thida and her children off the border.

Besides Thida's seven, there were many children in Mairut. Children made up roughly half the population in the border camps. They were a source of optimism and relief from the constant threats and worries. In a letter home, I described a typical encounter as it happened.

Mai Rut April 8, 1980

> *A little girl from the Khmer Rouge side of the camp has bravely ventured into the UNHCR building. Slowly and cautiously, she has worked her way up to the corner of my desk.*
>
> *"Sok sabai," I say softly, so as not to startle her. She smiles and blushes. "Chmu-ey? What is your name?"*
>
> *"Sary," she whispers.*
>
> *"Ah, Sary. Kyum chmu Scott."*
>
> *"Sco'." It's a difficult name for both Thai and Khmer to pronounce. She must be five or six. She is very cute.*
>
> *I then go back to my work, as there is work to be done. About five minutes later, the same little girl, who had remained at the corner of my desk, distracted me again.*
>
> *"Mui-bee-bai-bun..."*
>
> *She is now counting a stack of buckets in the corner. I say to her "Mui-bee-bai...One-two-three."*

"Wan-too-fwee."
I am refueled. Good for another eight hours at least.
The children. That's how we keep going. They give us our energy when the blistering sun has taken it away.

Seemingly unaffected by the starkness of their surroundings, the children would laugh, run, and play. The camp supplied their basic needs of food and shelter. They had all the attention of the underemployed adult population. Rather than see the closed world of the barbed wire that their parents saw, they saw only the free open space of the camp itself, their little world, where they would run in packs on the heels of the latest foreign visitor chanting "Okay. Bye-bye!"

Still, the children were not unaffected. The laughing bright faces of children with families were contrasted by the distant and withdrawn faces one encountered in the "Unaccompanied Minors" building—just three barracks down from Ly and Kolap. "Unaccompanied minors"—children, found up and down along the border, without parents. Missing parents. Dead parents. Even the faces with smiles had their stories. They had just managed to set them aside to deal with another day. Putting one foot in front of the other. No time to reflect. This is how children survive.

AFTER DARK

The COERR team stayed in the town of Trat, an hour north of the camp, but I really just wanted to stay in the camp with my friends. The two Thai Baptist volunteers had a small house outside the fence, and the MSF staffed the hospital overnight, but other than that, no foreigners were permitted in camp after dark. But if the Baptists and the MSF staff could stay overnight, why couldn't I?

I did not ask for permission.

At the end of one particular workday, I told my COERR team that I would hitch a ride back to town with another agency. Then, while I could still enter, I went to see Ly in Building 19. And there I stayed as night eventually came, and as the perimeter of the camp was secured for the night.

As the light dimmed with the setting of the sun over the Gulf of Siam, it was time for the evening bath. Ly demonstrated by bathing out in the open, scooping water with a bucket from an open well.

"Now you really see how we live."

I watched Ly deftly maneuver a rather thorough self-cleaning while maintaining his poise and dignity. Ly wore only his *khrama* as he bathed, a simple cloth called a sarong if worn by a woman and a *khrama* if worn by a man. Made of cotton or silk, it is wrapped around the body like a bath towel. It is an extremely versatile basic item of clothing. Women typically wear them as skirts. Men typically wear them at home. And everyone bathes in them.

When it was my turn, I changed into a borrowed *khrama* and went over to the well to bathe. I was less than confident that I had secured it and was worried that it would fall away at any moment.

As I started pouring water over myself, a large crowd gathered. While the modest and respectful nature of the Cambodians meant that Ly was able to bathe undisturbed, the spectacle generated by a white American boy bathing out in the open simply overwhelmed the usual decorum.

With a grin, and an adopted father's demeanor, Ly observed from a distance as I made my first awkward attempt to bathe in public. The crowd that assembled was growing by the minute, so in my embarrassment, I hastened to complete the job as quickly as possible. When I thought I had finished, Ly laughed and said, "You know, in Cambodia, we say a young man is not ready to marry if he does not know how to wash his body everywhere." This was in reference to the fact that, under the watchful gaze of so many observers, I had scrupulously avoided washing my private areas.

To be sure, I was not quite sure I could accomplish this simple task without dropping the wet *khrama* that clung to my hips and thighs. But Ly had challenged me in front of everyone, so I summoned the courage and quickly washed and rinsed my groin to howls and hoots of laughter. As I stood wrapped only in a wet *khrama* in the fading light of the camp, I felt all eyes upon me. Then I saw Kanya. She was laughing, along with all her siblings. And of all the times I had sought her attention, this was one time I could have done without it.

AT NINE O'CLOCK, the Thai military made an announcement over the loudspeaker. The commander summoned the Cambodian Section leaders to a meeting. Later, our house leader (one of my English students) returned to inform us that they were instructed to prepare for a possible attack. About a hundred Vietnamese soldiers had just crossed the border nearby and the Thai troops were taking up defensive positions.

I looked to Ly.

"We must wait to see what happens," he said. "We cannot go anywhere. The Thai guards will shoot us if we cross the fence. We must hope they can protect us. We have no freedom to do anything else."

The camp grew quiet and everyone was tense. The few lights were dimmed. Radios silenced. The usual talking and laughter ceased. From our vantage point, we could see Thai soldiers scrambling out of their barracks, clutching their rifles. Some climbed into jeeps that headed off to the road leading to the foot of the mountain; others went out on foot to take up defensive positions around the camp's barbed wire fences.

Then the military cut the main lights to the camp, apparently to conceal our location from Vietnamese artillery on the mountain.

We waited. I was nervous, but also a little excited. What would I do if they attacked us? What could we do? What about the children?

Ly and the rest took it all in stride. I could tell they took the alarm very seriously, but for them, it was just another day, just another threat to endure.

For the next hour, time passed slowly. The camp remained quiet and dark. The children had drifted off to sleep. There would be the occasional cough, or the cry of an infant, but for the duration, no one spoke above a whisper.

After an hour, the public address speaker crackled, "All clear!"

As the night progressed, we settled into the small area that was home for Ly and Kolap and Thida and the children. After dark, I saw a side of the camp I had never seen before. The same area that served as a gathering area, a food preparation area, and a study area was rapidly transformed into a sleeping area. Side by side and head to toe, the occupants occupied every inch of ground, sleeping on thin straw mats that hardly protected one from the sand flies that would nip and bite during the night.

Under the dim light of candles and lamps, after the chatter of relief following the "all clear" had subsided, a hush again fell over the camp. Cramped as quarters were, hushed voices came through the thin thatch walls and neighboring barracks fluttered in the gentle sea breeze. In the distance, a rare shortwave radio played a BBC broadcast in Khmer. Nearby, the sounds of an infant's cry could again be heard.

Kanya and Chanthy quietly studied and wrote in their paper notebooks by candlelight. The younger children had drifted off to sleep, one by one. When all the children were asleep, Ly, Kolap, and Thida sat with me. We continued to scheme about how we could secure their escape from the border to the safety of Canada or the US. We swapped stories of the day and made jokes to ease the tension. Thida gleefully reminded me of my awkward efforts bathing at the well and laughed, playfully slapping me on the shoulder.

Having changed into a dry *khrama* and T-shirt, I was growing tired. I was ready to sleep. Kolap and Thida prepared a space for me on the raised bamboo "bed" where the adults slept. Although I slept in a *khrama* like everyone else, I used my rolled up blue jeans as a pillow. They contained all my worldly wealth, on the order of fifteen dollars in Thai currency, and my passport. The border camps, including Mairut, were routinely harassed by shell fire, and the false alarm earlier in the evening made me uneasy. I didn't know about anyone else, but if one shell landed anywhere near the camp that night, my blue jeans and I were heading straight over that fence into the Gulf of Siam.

The rest of the night passed without incident. Despite all the excitement of the early evening, I felt at home. I was at peace. As I drifted off to sleep in the intimate makeshift home of my newly adopted family, I somehow felt more secure than I ever had before. I slept a deeper and more restful sleep than I had in years.

And yet, by living with my Cambodian friends, I was doing something that I was not supposed to do. The Thai camps were strictly run by the military, and access to the border was tightly regulated. The entire border was a military zone. Movements were strictly controlled, and special permits and passes were required to move about.

How I was able to get away with staying overnight in camp among the refugees remains a bit of a mystery, but my connections with Dang, the Thai UNHCR staffer, surely played a key role. Also, young as I was, with my T-shirts, blue jeans, and bare feet, I mostly moved below the radar. The young Thai guards who should have kicked me out after hours were more inclined to befriend a young American than to discipline him. So, after having managed to get myself "left behind" in camp the first time, I began staying overnight regularly. Not every night, as I was expected to spend some time with my team and also had to run errands for myself and my friends from time to time back in town. But I was lonely in my sparse hotel room back in town. I felt happiest when I was with my friends in camp, and I stayed overnight as often as I could.

I also was terribly naïve. I did not appreciate that what I was doing could lead to trouble. But the hours I spent with Ly, Kolap, and Thida in the dark of night in a remote border camp gave me the greatest opportunity to learn more about the culture and the history of my new friends and hear and learn from others in the camp as well. In the deep quiet of the late night, where the only sound was the hushed tones of quiet conversation in neighboring barracks, as the small children rolled out their straw mats and fell asleep at our feet, Cambodians came to Building 19 to share their survival stories with the American. They spoke quietly, reverently, as they told of family members who were killed by the Khmer Rouge, or who had died of illness, or starvation, or who had been taken away, never to return, their whereabouts unknown. Forced labor with long workdays—but they were allowed to take breaks to smoke home-rolled herbal cigarettes, so before long, everyone over age ten was a smoker.

They would look at me pleadingly, eyes swollen with tears, even as they came to understand there was little I could do to help them.

LY AND KOLAP SPOKE DESPONDENTLY about their young children, who they had not seen in nearly a year. They recounted the details of their flight across Cambodia. The starvation. The repatriations.

The moments when they had to wonder if they would ever make it to freedom. Kolap pointed to her well-worn thin rubber flip-flops. "These cheap shoes walked across the entire width of Cambodia! All the way from Vietnam!"

Thida would express her worry about her children and her future. Other refugees would politely present themselves, eager to unburden their own stories of suffering and survival. My presence provided some hope. They wanted to tell their stories to the young American.

They all spoke of the trauma from years under the Khmer Rouge and the fear of having to return to a Cambodia still at war. But they also spoke of their dreams, and although their more immediate dreams involved making it safely to a third country, they all dreamed of returning to a peaceful Cambodia someday.

They had many questions about America. Is it cold? Had I ever seen snow? Was everyone in the US rich and happy? Are all Americans fat like me?

Although my stays in the camps were voluntary, and I always had the freedom to leave, the experience was an eye-opener for me. I finally learned to bathe comfortably out in the open with nothing more than a *khrama* cloth around my waist, gathering the water in a small can from an open well. I slept in the narrow space Ly and Thida and their families made for me in their overcrowded end of the barracks. I learned to eat new foods, including spicy curries and soups with the feet and heads of the chicken floating among the noodles. Within days of arriving, however, my arms and legs were swollen and dotted with multiple mosquito bites. Ly and the others were intrigued by these bumps, as they did not have the same reaction. Within a week, my skin cleared, and I never reacted to a mosquito bite that way again.

LATER THE FOLLOWING DAY, for the first time, the refugees were allowed to leave the barbed wire camp and walk the short distance to the beach, where they all relaxed and swam for the rest of the day, as if the refugee camp over the bluff had vanished with all the worries associated with it. Many of the children, who had grown up in inland Cambodian provinces, had never been to the ocean, even though they now lived a matter of yards away.

As the sun set over the water, the soldiers, who had freely mixed and relaxed with the refugees, signaled that it was time to return to camp.

ALL THIS TIME, I continued to struggle to learn the Cambodian language, Khmer. With great patience, Ly and the others worked with me word by word, phrase by phrase. The one great advantage I had in learning Khmer over my friends in their efforts to learn English is that, while there were few native English speakers to learn with, there were dozens of willing Cambodian teachers. When one was too busy, others would be ready to repeat and repeat and listen and correct until my pronunciation approached the correct form.

I was not a natural with foreign languages. After six years of high school Spanish, I still struggled to construct a simple sentence because the whole thing was just a classroom exercise; it hadn't mattered to me. I had never applied myself to the task of learning Spanish as a means of communication. But I wasn't learning Khmer for a grade. Learning this new language now was essential. And in this full immersion environment, I developed rudimentary verbal skills rather quickly.

Although Ly was an able and often available interpreter, my rudimentary Cambodian language skills were the only way I could communicate directly with Thida and Kanya and most of the other refugees. Indeed, although Kanya had begun to learn English, and no doubt had a functioning vocabulary in English that exceeded mine in Khmer, her modesty kept her from ever speaking in English in my presence.

My inability to communicate with Thida should have been an impediment to our developing relationship, but so much seemed to happen on a deeper, nonverbal level. Thida was always so easygoing and could connect without words.

Like all refugees I met, Thida saw me as an opportunity to enlist a rare American ally in her effort to escape her perilous perch in a border camp. I knew that. But I felt like there was more to her friendship than just me as a lifeline. I felt it in the way she interacted with me with a kind of affection that seemed sincere, not manipulative. I was young, but not stupid. I felt it in my heart: her affection was genuine.

What she saw in me, I don't know. But she always seemed happy when I was with her. The bond that was forming seemed to be unbreakable.

On the Cambodian border in the early 1980s

In front of home the day before the accident, August 1972

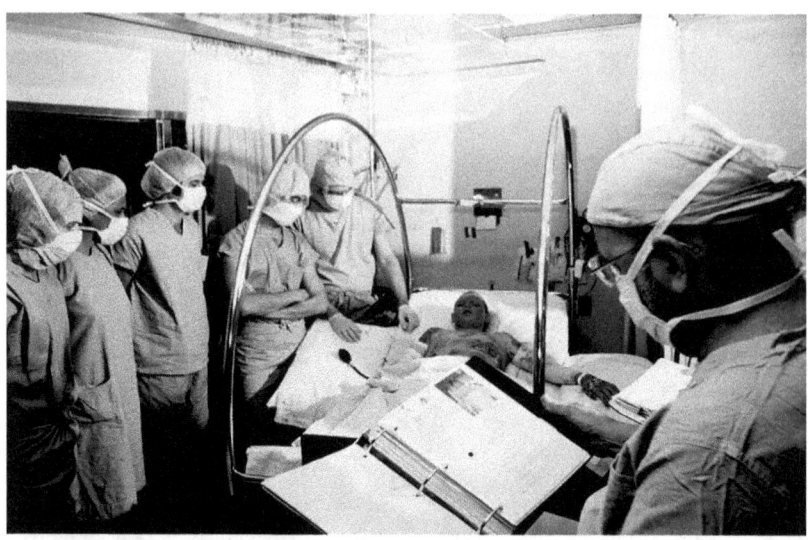

Shriner's burn unit in the 1970s, courtesy of Shriner's Hospitals for Children

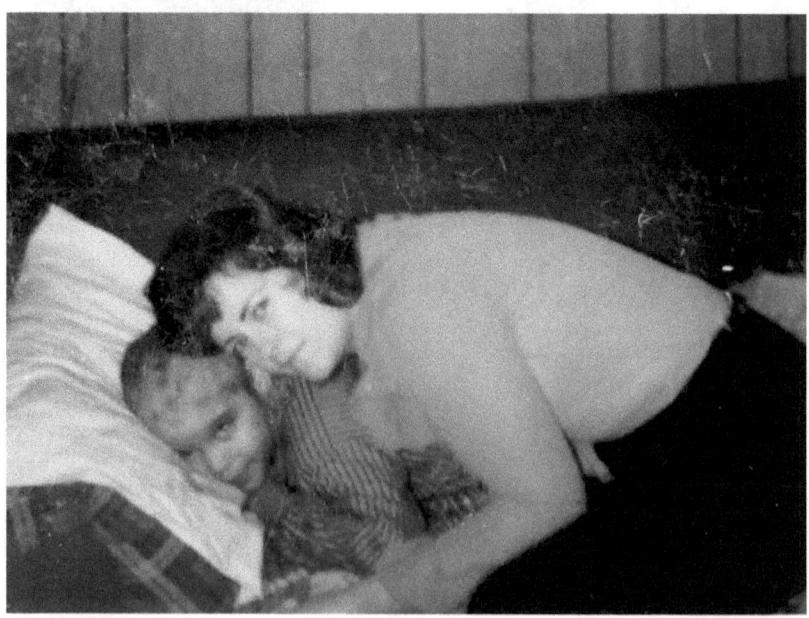

Rodney and his mother on his first day home from the Shriner's, 1972

The author with siblings, aunt, and uncle after release from the Shriner's, 1972

Ly standing very near the spot where we first met, Mairut Camp, March 1980

Kolap, Thida, and Kanya, Building 19, Mairut Camp, 1980

Thida and her children in Mairut Camp.
Back row: Tevy, Chanthy, Thida, Kanya, Vongsa.
Front row: Komar, Rasmey, and Malis.

COERR Mairut team, Trat, Thailand, 1980

David Lewis and Mai

Ly

Kolap

Thida

Clinic building at Mairut Camp gate

Young children at Mairut perimeter fence

Kanya

Playing guitar at Building 19

My parents visit Mairut Camp, July 1980

A special meal at Building 19

Interviewing Cambodian refugees for the Embassy

Sokhy, Kolap, and Ly in Chonburi Transit Camp

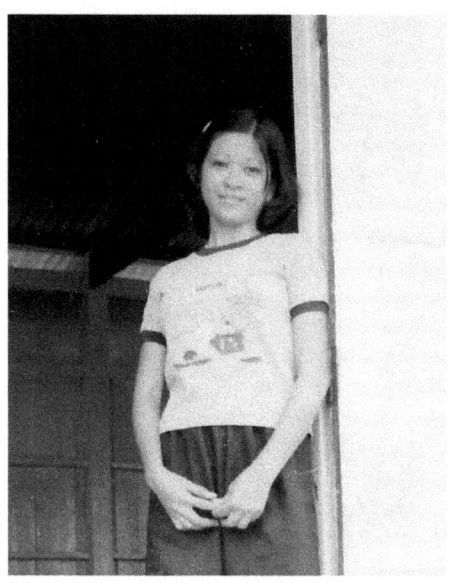

Minh Van, Songkhla Boat Camp

Minh Van on stage

Playing to a captive audience

With Minh Van, Songkhla Boat Camp 1980

With Quang, Songkhla Boat Camp

The Thai fishermen, Songkhla

Dennis Grace, US Embassy Refugee Section

US Embassy Refugee Section, Wireless Road, Bangkok

Kim Phuc, Burn Survivors of New England Meeting, Boston, 2010

Rodney

My family with Thida's surviving children, Long Beach, CA in 2019

Ly and Kolap, Phnom Penh, 2022

19

THE QUEEN VISITS

What the refugees in the camp needed was attention, and not just from me. For practical and emotional reasons, they needed the outside world to know of their plight. It was fortunate, then, that on occasion, we had high-profile visitors. Joan Baez and Rosalyn Carter had recently visited the larger camps to the north. To my great disappointment, I had missed *M*A*S*H* actor Mike Farrell's brief visit to Mairut on the only day I stayed behind in town because of an acute gastrointestinal illness, a common affliction of the relief workers adjusting to the local microbes.

One day, while I was working with a crew in Bamboo Camp setting up the outpatient building, moving the long bamboo shelves that would store the dispensary supplies, Dang pulled up in a jeep.

"Scott! Quick! I need you to come with me."

"What's up?" I set the shelf down. I excused myself and jogged over to Dang in the jeep.

"Just get in."

"Where are we going?"

"I can't tell you. Just come with me."

I hopped into the passenger seat and she pulled off, leaving a cloud of dust in our wake as we headed for the military compound.

ACROSS A BRIDGE OF FIRE

We parked the jeep, and without a word, Dang motioned for me to follow her towards a rapidly gathering group of soldiers and officers who were scrambling themselves into order. None of the other volunteer agency staff was present. I was puzzled.

Off in the distance, on the main road to Trat, I saw a short convoy of military trucks moving slowly south towards the entrance to Mai Rut. Approximately every twenty yards, a heavily armed soldier would jump out and take a position along the roadside. The trucks then made their way off the main road and up the camp road towards the military compound.

"What's going on?" I asked Dang.

"Just watch."

Shortly after the troops were in place along the road, a second group of trucks and jeeps came speeding down the main road and turned up the dirt road into camp, throwing dust high into the air. They pulled up right in front of us, and a group of soldiers emerged from the vehicles. The soldiers were excessively armed, with grenades, pistols, automatic rifles, and bandoliers.

Finally, I made out another small convoy that included two army jeeps flanking a white Mercedes with tinted glass windows. The soldiers fell into formation and stood at attention.

Dang, who stood to my left as we waited along the walkway that led to the camp commander's building, leaned over and whispered in my ear. "Now, just do as I do, and remember, your head should never be higher than the queen's."

The queen? Was this Sirikit, the Queen of Thailand? Why would she be here? Of course—she must have been at the Queen's Camp, Kao Larn, just to the north of us.

The king and queen of Thailand are highly revered and even considered semi-divine by many Thai people. I realized the presence of the queen on this rather insecure strip of the border was a bigger deal than the visits of foreign celebrities like Mike Farrell or Joan Baez.

No sooner had I pieced the puzzle together than the white Mercedes pulled up a few yards in front of us.

The door to the Mercedes was opened by a soldier who then bowed low. As Queen Sirikit stepped out into the bright sunshine, all the other soldiers snapped to attention and saluted.

She wore an olive-green uniform, one that had been clearly tailor-made to be sufficiently martial yet flattering. Following Dang's lead, I folded my hands together in the traditional "wai" of greeting, and we bowed our heads. She was a dignified woman in her late forties, with black hair, dark glasses, and pale skin that had obviously been well-protected from the unrelenting Thai sun.

The camp commander, Colonel Kosol, emerged from his office, saluted, and made his formal greetings before escorting the queen down the receiving line, which I now realized I was standing in.

Just then I became aware that I was dressed like a slob in my usual thong sandals, blue jeans, and a pale army green T-shirt.

"Dang," I whispered. "I'm not dressed appropriately!"

"Never mind! Too late!"

As the queen passed Dang and I, we bowed deeper, and the queen smiled and nodded. Our eyes met briefly, but I quickly looked down, unsure of whether I was worthy or whether it was appropriate to look directly at her. The queen and her party then disappeared into the commander's building, and we were left to wait, perhaps for thirty minutes, while she was given her orientation. We were not allowed to move. Dang explained, out of respect, we would remain in place until she came back. Then, in much the same manner as she had arrived, she emerged to everyone's strict attention, disappeared into the Mercedes, and took off to see other parts of the camp.

It was not clear to me why the queen had come to Mairut, other than the fact that her show camp for orphans was nearby. She did not stay long, and whatever conversations she had with the camp authorities happened outside of my earshot. She made no speeches. There was no formal ceremony. There apparently had been no advance notice of her visit.

Then, as quickly as she had arrived, the convoy of military vehicles and the Mercedes rolled away on the dirt road onto the main road— and she was gone.

We had not exchanged so much as a word, but I had been in the presence of a queen. In a refugee camp. I hadn't even dreamed of that happening. I thanked Dang for thinking of me, and she just smiled.

"No problem. I thought you would like to meet the queen!"

Why, I wondered, had Dang gone out of her way to pluck me out of camp for this rare opportunity to meet the queen? Surely there were more important people in the camp—doctors, nurses, teachers. Later, I asked her. She explained that she shared these gifts with me because, more than most visitors and workers in the camps in those days, she saw that I wanted so much to learn about and know the new cultures I was immersed in. She reminded me that she had invited me to dinner one night in town with the governor of Trat province for the same reason. She gave me these gifts because she knew I would value them more than anyone else.

The queen's visit also gave me the gift of hope for my Cambodian friends. Even though no embassies had come to the camp, the queen had. If the queen would visit, how much longer could these people go unnoticed?

BORDER THREATS

Mairut Camp was in a quieter part of the border. Most of the fighting was centered around the Khmer Rouge and non-communist resistance strongholds to the north. Still, our camp was in a precarious location on the low ground bounded by the ocean. The Queen's Camp, even with its large red crosses, had come under shell fire not long after the queen's visit.

One morning, following one of my rare nights staying with my team in the town of Trat, the soldiers stopped us as we arrived at the camp. There was more activity at the gate than usual. Near the camp perimeter, a group of soldiers gathered around a small crater in the ground in between the Old Camp and the Bamboo Camp. Our driver asked the soldier at the gate what was going on. The soldier said the camp had been shelled during the night. One shell had landed near the entrance to the camp in a field just outside the fence. Apparently, no one had been injured.

We paused, and we all craned our necks to look over at the crater. It was only about a hundred yards from the closest barracks of the camp, where unarmed men, women, and children—my friends—had been sleeping.

Ly, Kolap, Thida, the children. I was eager to check on my friends.

ACROSS A BRIDGE OF FIRE

When I reached them, they were indeed unharmed, but they were rattled. Ly recounted how they were all awakened by a loud boom. I had never seen him angry before, but he was angry now. The soldiers had not allowed the refugees to flee from the camp despite their pleas for permission to move away from the incoming fire. They had hoped to at least move beyond the bluff on to the beach where they would have been less at risk and free to flee north or south or at least disperse, but when Ly led the refugees in his section to the gate of the camp, the Thai soldiers held them back at gunpoint.

"How could they stop us? They aim their guns at us and shout for us to stay behind the wire. How can they do that?" Ly shook his head. "They would not open the gate, and we have nothing to cut the wire fence in an emergency."

The very next day, I reentered the camp with a pair of wire cutters I had purchased from a hardware store in town tucked under a *khrama*. Ly had never explicitly asked me for them, and he was surprised when I presented them, but he quickly took them and hid them among his belongings. Cutting the wire and escaping from the camp could only have been attempted under extreme duress. Ly knew this. The young and sometimes trigger-happy Thai guards had shot, injured, and even killed refugees caught fleeing from the camps. We had only just learned in a camp briefing that a refugee had been shot and killed as he ran out the main gate of the large camp of Khao I Dang—just yards away from the UNHCR field office and in front of international aid workers.

Things changed quickly from day to day on the border, and after a few days with no further shelling or Vietnamese incursions nearby, security was relaxed again.

In mid-April, it was Cambodian New Year, which coincides with the Thai water festival, Songkran, which also marks the new year. I had been in Mairut for a little over a month. In Bamboo Camp, there was a formal ceremony marking Songkran, as well as the opening of a new school building for the children. The ceremony began formally, with the refugee leaders demonstrating their gratitude to the Thai military, UNHCR, and volunteer agency staff by ceremoniously pouring water over their hands. But as time went on, and the celebration moved further away from the dignitaries and into the crowd, the formal sprinkling of water progressed to splashing of water, and eventually, to an all-out water fight.

Following the opening ceremony, the commander announced that the refugees would be permitted to leave the compound and spend the day at the beach. His decision to allow the refugees to exit the barbed-wire camp again was well received (especially since no one had been allowed out when the camp was under attack).

At the beach, we waded into the warm, clear blue water. No one, including myself, had proper swimming attire, so we all simply waded into the Gulf of Siam fully clothed or, for the men, with shirts off. The small children stripped naked.

Thida's children splashed in the shallow water and laughed as they ran along the water's edge. The older people cautiously waded into the shallow gulf waves, searching the clear, light blue water for jellyfish.

For this special event, even the young Thai soldiers loosened up. Off-duty soldiers lingered among the Cambodians, playing drums and guitars, singing, sharing food and fruit, laughing and sharing stories with the refugees who understood Thai—as if it were a day at a normal beach resort, although this beach was far from any resort and was bounded by minefields.

I received several nasty jellyfish stings in the clear, warm water, but that seemed a small price to pay for such a rare and memorable day at one of the world's most inaccessible and pristine tropical beaches. We all laughed and sang until the beach day was cut short by a sudden intense downpour of rain that sent us scattering back to the camp. Getting caught in a torrential downpour is part of life in Southeast Asia, and we laughed as we ran back to Building 19 where we shed our soaked salty clothes in favor of *khramas* and sarongs. There we reclined, winded from our dash through the rain, processing the fresh memories of an unanticipated day of relative freedom and lightness.

Freedom and lightness were precious, but carefree moments

passed quickly on the border. Nothing is permanent. Mere days after the beach celebration, trouble returned.

About a week later, as my team arrived at the camp one morning, there was again a crowd of soldiers near the gate, much like we had seen after the shelling. Only this time, the soldiers were grimmer. They were surveying the ground around a Toyota sedan with a shattered windshield that sat slightly off the road. They pointed from the car to the surrounding ground, speaking to each other and shaking their heads.

Our driver rolled down his window and called to the guard at the gate.

"What's going on?" I asked.

A soldier approached the driver's side of our van and began speaking to the driver in Thai. I leaned in to see if I could understand anything he was saying. I couldn't. My Thai wasn't up to it.

Our driver shook his head and sighed. He turned to me.

"Colonel Kosol was shot. Last night."

"What?"

"Shot. Killed. *Bup-bup-bup!* Shot through his windshield." He held his hands as if shooting an automatic rifle and then pointed towards the damaged vehicle. "Oh, very bad!"

Colonel Somsak Kosol, the camp commander, had been assassinated as he left camp the night before. An unidentified female companion was also killed.

In the van, the nuns and I looked at each other.

"Is it still safe for us to be here?" one of them asked.

Apparently, the camp commander himself was not safe in this Thai-held and Thai-controlled territory on the border.

Although my impression of the colonel was that he was a stern and aloof officer, my friend Dang had explained that Kosol was compassionate towards the refugees and extremely intolerant of exploitation and corruption by those who might take advantage of them. As in any other wartime environment, while people suffered, unethical locals saw the opportunity to profit from their refugees and from the resources flowing in from international agencies. Kosol had thwarted many of their efforts, a principled stand that eventually led to the well-planned ambush as he left the camp.

Colonel Kosol and his companion were killed by gunfire as they turned onto the main road at the main entrance to the camp, the same road we used every day—the same road the queen herself had traveled only weeks earlier. The perpetrators had used AK-47s in order to create the appearance of a Cambodian or Vietnamese attack. But that fooled no one. Neither the Vietnamese nor the Khmer Rouge had assassinated Kosol, and the story in the next day's *Bangkok Post* acknowledged as much. Kosol was killed by his own countrymen.

The assassination shocked everyone. It reminded all of us that the Thai-Cambodian border really was the wild west. In the coming hours and days, we all tried to process the news. We had only started feeling somewhat safe with the daily routine of work on the border. But on the border, there was no enduring safety.

Kosol's sudden and violent death devastated Dang. Dang had been close to Kosol through her work as the Thai liaison for the UNHCR, and she enjoyed the blessings of his favor in the relative freedom she had in her many activities in the camp. That relationship had benefited me as well. There is little doubt that my free movement about the camps would not have been tolerated had Dang not vouched for me with the colonel.

Dang was shaken. I had never even seen her upset before. She always seemed so carefree. In the immediate aftermath of the killing, she kept up a strong front in public. But in private, her eyes quickly filled with tears. That night back at the Trat Hotel, she instructed me to meet her in her room. Once we were alone, she confided to me that she feared for her life.

"The people who killed my friend might want to kill me, too!"

Dang's boyfriend was a police officer who lived and worked in another province. He made occasional weekend visits to Trat whenever he could. Even before Kosol's assassination, he had become concerned for Dang's safety, and he had given her a revolver to keep for her personal protection.

As a UN worker, Dang could not carry a weapon into camp, so she left the handgun in an unsecured cabinet in her hotel room. That night, as we sat together on the bed of her dimly lit room, her eyes filled with tears. She looked up at me.

"You must be very careful, too," she began. "I can no longer assure you that you are safe. I mean it. You must be very careful."

She removed the revolver from the cabinet and held it in her hands. "I don't want you to touch this. But I want you to know where it is," she whispered. "I do not know what may happen in the next few weeks. But if you are ever in trouble—or if anything happens to me—I want you to know where this is."

The look on her face made me uncomfortable. She wasn't joking. She held out the gun to me.

"Do you know how to use a gun?"

I looked down at the floor.

"I hope I never have to," I said, and I tried to smile in an attempt to make light of the situation.

"I'm serious. I'm not joking!" Her eyes widened. Her expression was intense, nothing like the disarming smile she normally displayed. "The people who killed Kosol are in charge of the camp now. They know I was his friend, and you are my friend. Just be very careful. And, please, don't talk to anyone about this. This is just between us!"

I wanted to say something comforting, something reassuring. But I had no words.

I had not been entirely naïve about the dangers of the border, and as a burn survivor, I knew it was all a bit of a crapshoot anyway. But this gangland threat was not the kind of thing I had expected. I was just a refugee worker, after all. If I was in danger, it should be related to the expected risks of a war zone. A landmine or a stray shell. Malaria, even. But not this.

The week that followed was tense. Dang, who previously had status, privilege, and the run of Mairut Camp under Colonel Kosol, tiptoed around on eggshells under the watchful eyes of the new military leaders. I plowed myself into my daily routine of teaching English to the teachers at the new school and tried to lie low. In the days following Kosol's death, even I understood that I should not try to sneak into camp after dark, and I did my best not to attract any attention.

Time passed.

Nothing happened to Dang.

Nothing happened to me.

The gun in Dang's cabinet was never mentioned again.

As more days passed with no repercussions, Dang and I began to feel a tentative sense of relief.

After that, Dang never raised the subject again. Another threat had passed. No time to reflect. Just keep going.

At the next weekly UNHCR meeting in the bamboo hut, Stephan acknowledged the assassination. By then, we had all discussed it among ourselves, and there wasn't much new to add. He then turned to ongoing threats.

"As you all know, the Vietnamese and their enemies, the remnants of the Khmer Rouge, are all along the border. We are on that border. Fortunately, at present, all the fighting and heavy shelling are to the north.

"At border camp 204, internal fighting among Khmer Serei factions recently left thirty civilians dead, and one hundred wounded. Not long after that, the Vietnamese shelled the camp. The closest fighting to us is about three miles north of us at Khao Larn, the 'Queen's Camp,' the show camp supported by the Queen of Thailand for orphans. That camp, like Mairut, was located at the foot of the border mountains. Fighting between the Khmer Rouge and the Vietnamese was a more common occurrence at Khao Larn, even though Mairut also presented an easy target.

"The main Khmer Rouge camps are further up north, a few hours away. The objective of the Vietnamese forces is to wipe out the remnants of the Khmer Rouge. So, I suppose as long as the Vietnamese are busy fighting the Khmer Rouge to the north, they'll be too busy to come in our direction. The Queen's Camp was shelled again last night, but there were no injuries," Stephan concluded. "If anything changes, I will let you all know immediately. Everyone needs to be on alert and be ready to respond to instructions by our new camp commander if anything happens here. Remember, the military are here to keep us safe."

The assembled volag workers erupted in a skeptical groan.

The assassins are here to keep us safe?

IN THOSE DAYS, what I knew of the larger northern border camps came down through the refugees and other relief workers, including our own team members, who traveled through from time to time, and from what I read in stories about those camps in the *Bangkok Post*.

One weekend, however, a month or so after I had arrived in Mairut, David Lewis invited me to accompany him on a short trip to the border area around Aranyaprathet up north. He wanted to show me a bit of the main stage of operations on the border. Once again, I had the privilege of a ride in his air-conditioned chauffeured Mercedes as we headed north.

From the comfort of that vehicle, I saw some of the most unforgettable scenes I had witnessed to date. We drove past a Thai tank division and artillery units on the road. I had never seen tanks or artillery before, let alone in a war zone. There must be fighting nearby, David said. As we drew closer to the border, we came upon an open field with literally thousands of refugees, possessions on their backs and heads, making their way through the dusty landscape, surrounded by Thai troops who were guiding their movement. A mass of humanity, as far as the eye could see.

"There's been more shelling," David said. "They're moving deeper in country. When it settles down, they'll move back." The sheer number of people and the expanse of the scene struck me, as I had seen nothing like this further south. It was like a scene from a movie.

When I first saw Khao I Dang Camp, I was overwhelmed by its size. It went on forever. The population well exceeded 150,000, making it possibly the second largest Cambodian city of the time (Phnom Penh being first.) The Red Cross (ICRC) hospital was huge, and the number of agencies and workers impressed me. UN and international agency trucks came and went through the main gate, and the rows of bamboo barracks stretched back as far as the eye could see. In the main hospital, we saw many patients with newly amputated limbs from injuries sustained on the heavily mined border. There were many more patients sick with malaria, tuberculosis, dengue fever, and gastrointestinal illnesses.

We made brief stops at Sakeo and another border camp, and then made our way back to the Aranyaprathet Thai-style wooden house where our team was quartered. There, I would bunk down for the night. David, as usual, had secured an air-conditioned room somewhere else in town.

The Khao I Dang COERR team impressed me. This was the largest team COERR had fielded at the time; there were four doctors and seven or eight nurses. Since my own hospitalization, I had dreamed of becoming a doctor, so I eagerly questioned them about their work. They just as eagerly questioned me. "How the hell did you get here? You mean you don't even have first aid training?"

People came and went constantly throughout the night; there was a sense of chaos and urgency, as well as recklessness. After a brief chat, several of the male doctors excused themselves to head for a small frontier Thai bar and go-go club, to the consternation of their female coworkers.

I slept that night on a thin mat on the floor, listening to the distant thumping of outgoing shelling. I was on the razor's edge.

Following an uneasy night's sleep, I awoke early the next morning to return to Trat in David's air-conditioned Mercedes.

COMPASSION FATIGUE

We had survived the threat of Vietnamese incursion and an assassination, but COERR would not survive the vagaries of international relief politics. In early May, two months after my arrival in camp, word came down from Bangkok that COERR was winding down its border operations. COERR had already pulled teams from Sakeo, Kamput, and Khao I Dang. They would phase out the Mairut operation in the coming weeks.

I had not seen this coming.

Just when my new friends and their fellow refugees needed the most help, someone changed the channel. The seasoned refugee workers referred to waning support from the US and the Western world at large as "compassion fatigue." The world was tuning out from the Cambodian story. For about six months, the border situation had dominated the international headlines. But by May, the crisis level publicity was tapering off, as were donations and funding.

Despite ongoing security threats, work in the camps was also becoming more settled, and the first inevitable steps towards bureaucratization of the refugee work were being taken. Gone were the days of showing up and pitching in together. The roles for each volunteer agency were now meticulously negotiated and the boundaries of every agency's work jealously guarded. The major roles of health care, nutrition, education, and skills training had been divvied up among the larger international relief agencies. Smaller, well-meaning but resource-constrained agencies like COERR were fighting over scraps. David warned us during his last visit that things were always fluid, and it was unclear how long our services would be needed in the camp. But I just couldn't accept that we would walk away from the refugees of Mairut Camp.

A week later, Mai arrived from Bangkok without David. David was gone. He had been called back to the US.

The Mariel Boatlift was now underway. The Castro regime had allowed Cubans to flee communist Cuba to the United States, and tens of thousands did, arriving by small boats on the Florida coast. Suddenly, American eyes were diverted from a faraway human residuum of a war they had lost in Asia towards boatloads of Cubans arriving on American shores.

ICMC (the international arm of COERR) had summoned David back home to lead the effort to process the Cuban refugees that were arriving at Fort Chaffee, Arkansas. David had coordinated the resettlement of evacuated Vietnamese refugees at Fort Chaffee following the fall of Saigon in 1975, so they figured he was the man for the job—never mind the Cambodians.

Mai informed us that COERR was shutting down its Mairut border program immediately. Everyone on the team was to pack up, and a van would shuttle us to Bangkok the following day. We would all be sent back to the US within the coming weeks.

After only two months, my time as a relief worker in Mairut was over.

COERR was a small agency. The other agencies already in the camp would easily pick up their work. So, while my job was vanishing, the refugees weren't going anywhere and the work supporting them would continue, just with more limited support.

The diversion of attention from the Cambodian border crisis created by the Cuban boat flotilla was deeply frustrating to me. Although Cambodians remained in danger and in limbo, the news cycle had moved on. As this new reality settled in, I became increasingly pessimistic. As Western attention receded, the very real specter of forced repatriation back to Cambodia increased.

Newspapers and the BBC reported the failed effort to supply the Cambodian interior with much needed food rations. A famine was underway in the country. Ongoing fighting between the Vietnamese and the remnants of the Khmer Rouge prevented the annual rice crop harvest, and political and security barriers prevented planned delivery of relief aid from the international community, whether by air, land, or sea. From the border, we watched with feelings of impotence as the specter of another round of famine developed. The Cambodians on the border were clinging on, trying their very best not to fall—or be pushed back—into the abyss.

Just as I was losing my position, everything seemed like it was getting worse for the Cambodians. I was not ready to leave. Not now.

But without work, my visa would soon expire. I would be bound to not only leave Mairut, but the country entirely.

"You could just stay here with us," Ly said, on learning the news. "We would be happy for you to just stay here on your own."

"I would be happy too, Ly," I replied. "But the Thai would never let me do it."

I was determined to find a way to stay. I had grown attached to the families of Ly and Thida and could not imagine leaving them.

Ly had turned so many bad situations into good. He continued to be optimistic.

"You will find another job. And if you have to go to Bangkok, you can visit the Australian and Canadian embassies again and check on our applications for resettlement with them."

Thida was more worried about the prospect of my leaving, but disguised her concern in her usual manner through gentle teasing.

"Scott will go to Bangkok, find a girlfriend, and forget all about us!"

"I won't forget you Thida," I replied in Khmer.

"Scott, please don't forget Thida!" She said it with a smile. But I could tell she was not joking.

By the time I made it to the COERR house in Bangkok, I was in for another rude awakening. David had always offered the house as a base for his relief workers when they were in town. But he was gone. In his place was a formal, thin man with wire-rimmed glasses and a crew cut named John Cullen. From the moment I knocked on the door, John, who now occupied the COERR house with his wife and children, seemed uncomfortable to have me in the home.

John had come to Thailand under the auspices of ICMC not to oversee relief work on the border, but to help the US embassy launch a brand-new program for Vietnamese refugees. In order to stem the flow of refugees fleeing by boat, the US and Vietnamese governments were attempting to set up a refugee processing path that would enable those wishing to leave Vietnam to stay in Vietnam while their applications for resettlement were considered. If approved, they would travel by air to the US. This program was called the Orderly Departure Program (ODP).

John arrived expecting to help launch ODP, not wind down a Cambodian border relief operation. He was just as surprised as us to find himself thrust into the position, and he seemed eager to do it quickly.

Other American COERR workers had arrived at the house from other camps in an effort to figure out what was going on. Everyone was upset and agitated. An older woman who had been a volunteer for COERR at Khao I Dang was emotional and could not stop crying. Events had pushed her over the edge. She said she felt she was at the point of breakdown. The border was evil and violent. She fretted about how unpredictable everything was. Worrying about the people she had met, she wondered if they would survive.

I awkwardly offered words of comfort, but they fell flat. Inside, I had no patience for her frailty. To myself, I thought, at times like this, you cannot break down. You do what you have to do and sort it out later. Much later. For better or worse, that is what I had learned at a young age from my grandfather, my father, and the fire chief,

Ken Drs. You have to *compartmentalize*, just to function, to survive. Reflection must wait. You have to keep going. You cannot stop. In the heat of the moment, there is no time to reflect!

I HAD TO FIND A JOB, and fast. I started knocking on doors. I applied at every volunteer agency in Thailand that was working on the border. I applied to be an ambulance driver for the International Committee for the Red Cross. I applied to the Thai Baptist Mission. My Thai Baptist friends from Mairut, Bill and Bruce, had sent me to their in-country headquarters with a supportive letter. "We are all here doing God's work," they wrote, and said they would be delighted if I joined their team in Mairut. But the Thai Baptist Mission's Bangkok office turned me down—because I was not Baptist. I applied to the International Rescue Committee. I was politely received everywhere, but in spite of two months' experience on the border, I was still basically a kid with no skills or credentials. I had been very fortunate to get that first job.

Things looked grim.

I made one last stop at the Refugee Section of the US embassy. There was not much hope of the US embassy hiring a seventeen-year-old high school dropout with two months' experience on the border, but I wasn't going to give up without exhausting all my options.

I entered the same refugee offices on Wireless Road where I had first met David Lewis. A Thai staffer had me fill out a standard employment application and told me to take a seat.

Rick Barnes, an affable young administrator for the Joint Voluntary Agency (JVA), the contract agency that handled refugee processing under the auspices of the US State Department, came down to the lobby to meet me, quickly reviewed my very short application, and gave me an even shorter interview on the spot.

"Well," he said, "I don't think I need anyone now, but, you know, feel free to check back in a week or so."

I HAD SOME TIME TO KILL. Even though my parents had filed sponsorship papers, nothing had happened. The US Embassy was not coming to the border camps, and Cambodian refugees were not being processed for resettlement. But a few other countries had processed a small number of applicants. I went by the Australian and Canadian embassies to check on the status of Ly's applications. Ly had worked as an interpreter with both country delegations when they had visited the border, and there was a chance they might look upon his application for resettlement favorably. Both embassies were polite, but noncommittal.

I took the opportunity to explore Bangkok, really, for the first time since my initial arrival. Given the cheapness of the un-air-conditioned bus system, I rode aimlessly to the far corners of the sprawling city, from the base of Sukhumvit to the provincial bus station, to New Petchburi Road, past Democracy Monument into the old city, near the Grand Palace and the Sanam Luang where the great weekend market took place, over to Chinatown, and back to the Siam Square area of Rama I Road.

In Siam Square, behind several large movie houses that showed Western films with English soundtracks, was a bookstore called D.K. Books that Richard Neharry, the American I had shared my first few days with, had introduced me to.

I was so bored I found myself poking around the textbook section. I saw a section called "Managing/Sales." I decided to see if they had any of the books my dad used in his college classes. And there, on the shelf in the D.K. bookstore, was a copy of *Retailing*, written by Robert F. Spohn and Robert Y. Allen, my father.

I looked around me. I wanted to say "Hey, look! My father's book!"

There was no one. No one to share my excitement with. And at that moment, I felt completely alone.

I flipped open the book and read the preface. At the end, my dad thanked my mom for her support and my grandmother for typing the manuscript. Damn. There they were. My family, in a familiar book in this faraway place. I felt a wave of emotion.

I missed them.

Loneliness, and specifically, the complete isolation and distance from my family and high school friends—albeit a self-imposed situation—was hard for me. Phone calls were too expensive, and the connections were poor. Letters took weeks. I didn't know any Americans or even Europeans in Thailand who were my age. Still, I had gotten myself into this situation. I would just have to deal with it.

I was in a city of over five million, yet I was alone. Though I felt a deep kinship with Ly, Kolap, and Thida, and was at complete peace when I was with them, when I was outside the camp, I was often alone. While I believed I could survive on my own, I didn't like being alone.

I took solace in knowing my family now supported what I was doing. And I knew, despite the separation, I was always on their mind.

My spiritual beliefs were rooted heavily in my family relationships. Having been raised a New England Congregationalist, I believed in God. I can't really explain it, but during my hospitalization for my burns, where I also was often separated from my family, I always felt the presence and the warmth of God. That feeling of God's love I first felt on the burn ward never left me.

Still, I had trouble relating to the concept of a faceless God. That God was too abstract. So, while I did feel God's presence, I also found comfort in thinking about two of my closest relatives who had passed away: my father's mother, Nana, who had died four years after my accident, and my mother's aunt, Pauline, who had died just before I left for Thailand. I believed they were with me and were watching over me when I was otherwise alone or in danger. So, while I was intensely lonely in the conventional sense when I was in Bangkok, I never felt like I was completely alone. I felt my ancestors watching over me. As I learned more about the customs and culture of Southeast Asia, I learned that many people practiced forms of ancestral veneration or worship alongside more traditional Buddhist rituals. It made all the sense in the world to me and further reassured me that I had found my tribe.

John Cullen had booted me out of the COERR house, so I returned to the low budget Atlanta Hotel where I had spent my first night in Thailand. There I read cheap paperbacks picked up in the lobby and wrote long letters to friends in the US with the hope they might write me back. I knew that I was drifting away from my high school friends, and that there always had been a certain gap that divided us. But I still missed them.

I read Hemingway's *A Farewell to Arms*. I read the *Bangkok Post* with war news from the border, Afghanistan, and Central America. I grew increasingly despondent because I was reminded of how suffering is everywhere and there was really nothing I could do to change it.

Still, while I was pessimistic about being able to make any meaningful changes in my new world, when I looked back at my life in Connecticut, I knew I didn't want to go back. All I could see was this huge, wide-open sky and this wild, exotic universe that was my new life in Thailand. And my sense of obligation to help the Cambodians had only deepened. I was sober about the odds, but I had neither given up hope nor lost resolve.

THE FOLLOWING WEEK, I returned to the US Embassy Refugee Section and was again greeted by Rick Barnes.

"If you are willing to work as a volunteer," he said, "I think we can use you. But the embassy is not allowed on the Cambodian border at this time. The Thai are still pushing for repatriation of the Cambodians and don't want us to raise their hopes of resettlement. But we could use you in the Vietnamese boat section."

As a volunteer, I would get a stipend of twenty-five dollars each week. The embassy would provide meals, work related transportation, and a place to stay.

I needed to get back to the border. While this wouldn't get me there directly, it was too good an offer to refuse.

Before the following day had ended, I was holding a freshly laminated official photo I.D. card in my hands:

Scott Allen
American Embassy, Bangkok

Well. If my friends could see me now.

EMBASSY WORKER

The next morning, Rick led me downstairs to the office of Dennis Grace, a bright and determined man in his early thirties who headed the Vietnamese boat dection. The "boat section," of the embassy Refugee Section was tasked with interviewing and processing Vietnamese refugees who had reached Thai shores in cramped, overcrowded boats.

Dennis was no nonsense. He immediately impressed me. He was knowledgeable, confident, assertive, and had a profound sense of mission. He had lived in northern Thailand and Laos following a stint in the air force in the early seventies during the Vietnam War. After completing his masters in Asian studies at Harvard, he returned to Thailand with his Laotian wife and their five-year-old daughter to work in the refugee program.

After providing me with a brief orientation to the Vietnamese refugee situation in Thailand, Dennis told me I was to be on a plane to Hadyai in southern Thailand the following Monday. There, I would meet up with Larry Crider, a former Peace Corps volunteer. Together, we would be the embassy team for the Vietnamese refugee camp at Songkhla, a fishing village in southern Thailand.

Never one to have enough good judgment to hold my tongue,

I told Dennis that, while I was honored to have this opportunity to help the Vietnamese, I had unfinished business and commitments to people on the Cambodian border and would prefer to return there as quickly as possible. I told him about Ly, Kolap, and Thida. Although I understood that all the refugee groups—the Hmong, the lowland Lao, the Vietnamese, and the Cambodian—were compelling, I felt the Cambodian situation was the most urgent. In any event, I had made promises to my Cambodian friends.

Dennis listened. He said he understood. But there were things I needed to understand.

"The Vietnamese who are arriving on Southeast Asian shores by boat are also in a very precarious position. Most boats have been sacked by Thai pirates. Most of the women have been raped by the time they reach Thai soil. Many of the boats are being pushed out to sea, and many are sinking with their human cargo."

Dennis explained how, for both political and cultural reasons, the Thai really did not like the idea of Vietnamese people on their soil and there was an opportunity to move them out quickly. He pointed out that the refugees now included growing numbers of high-ranking former military and government officials who were emerging from reeducation camps in Vietnam, people for whom the US had a compelling obligation and responsibility to help.

Finally, he made the point that in times of crisis, it is not a contest. Both the Vietnamese and the Cambodians in Thailand needed help. It just so happened that the embassy had access to the Vietnamese population at this time. The Cambodians were off limits to the embassy. And we had to work with the opportunities we had.

It was an unassailable argument, and I had no rebuttal. The Cambodians would have to wait. No amount of advocacy on my part for my friends would have any influence on the US State Department's negotiations with the Royal Thai Government and the Thai military regarding third country resettlement for Cambodians on the border. For now, my mission would be helping the large number of Vietnamese refugees arriving daily on Thai shores.

Dennis had shown me the location of Songkhla on a wall map of

Thailand. It was way, way down south, near Malaysia, about as far away from Mairut as one could get and still be in Thailand. It would take at least twenty-six hours by bus to travel between the two places.

I was scheduled to be on a Thai Airways flight to southern Thailand the following Monday. I still had the weekend. So, I grabbed the late-night bus for the six-hour journey to Trat Friday night and hitched a ride into Mairut the next morning with some former colleagues from CONCERN. I was already known to the perimeter guard, and my credentials were not even requested. The security situation appeared to be relaxed, so I took the opportunity to stay in camp with my friends.

That night, after all the relief workers had left the camp for the night, I went out for an evening walk in camp with Ly and Kolap. At one point, we strayed too close to the fence, and we were spotted by a Thai soldier who I had not met before. He called out to us shouting something in Thai, which Kolap understood.

"He says he wants us to go over there." We walked over, and I was immediately detained and escorted to the nearest guardhouse while the soldier radioed to his commander. Ly and Kolap stood anxiously nearby.

We waited. There was some movement over at the military barracks, and I saw the commander walk out, climb into a jeep, and head our way.

Only months ago, my alliance with Dang and Kosol would have rendered me immune to any consequences. But Kosol was dead, and many of the young soldiers who knew me from before were gone. It turns out I had just gotten lucky on arrival at the gate. But my luck had run out.

I only had two forms of identification on me: a US passport, and a United States embassy official I.D. card. I did not have any of the required documentation or clearance from the Thai military permitting me to be in that part of the country, let alone within the refugee camp, especially after hours.

The commander arrived and looked me up and down. I thought of how my fellow COERR relief worker, the Reverend Peter Pond, had been thrown in the stockade when he was caught bringing unauthorized supplies into another border camp to the north earlier that year. (Years later, on a similar run, he would be shot in the leg).

I began to sweat. I had screwed up, and I knew it.

Through Kolap, the commander informed me I would be detained in the military compound.

At this point, seeing no other option, I reached into my pocket and pulled out my American embassy I.D. The embassy I.D. card surprised him. But it didn't help like I thought it would.

US embassy? Why was I there? On what business? On whose authority? Why were we not informed?

Kolap, who spoke some Thai, did all the fast talking. She said I was not there on official business. She told the commander that I had merely come for a visit with old friends and had missed my ride back to town. At that point, the commander softened a bit. He offered for me to sleep in the military barracks with his troops as a guest, not a detainee. In the morning, I would have to leave camp and not return. I was more than willing to accept this compromise as a generous alternative to the stockade, but Kolap spoke up again.

"Look at him; he is just a boy. He will be too frightened to stay with soldiers. He knows us. We will look after him."

To my complete surprise, the commander allowed me to stay in the camp. I had dodged another bullet.

Later that night, as quiet settled over the camp, I shared my mixed feelings about my new job with the embassy with Ly, Kolap, and Thida.

"I think that taking this job with the embassy has put me in a good position to help your cases for resettlement," I began, "but I wish I could stay with you here in the camp."

"Scott, we will miss you," Kolap said. "But you need to have a job, or they won't let you stay. Go to the new job, and you can help us from there. Then we will all be together again in the future in a free country."

"But will you still visit us sometime?" Thida asked, looking less reassured than Ly and Kolap.

"Yes, Thida," I replied. "I will come whenever I can."

SONGKHLA CAMP

I flew to southern Thailand where I was met by Larry Crider, the former Peace Corps volunteer and conscientious objector during the Vietnam War. The camp was located on a beach, literally on the edge of the water, not set back from it like Mairut was. Songkhla Camp was small and dirty, with long grey wooden barracks lined up perpendicular to the shore. It had been thrown together next to a fish sauce factory, and the stench of dead fish was inescapable.

Compared to the Cambodian land camps with their populations in the tens of thousands, Songkhla was small—roughly seven thousand refugees at any given point. The population was lower in large part because third countries were interviewing and accepting Vietnamese refugees for resettlement at a quick pace. Still, the camp was overcrowded in that it held double its planned capacity of residents.

My job was to register and conduct the initial interviews of refugee applicants applying for asylum in the US. Basically, that included the entire population of the camp. Larry patiently introduced me to the forms and guided me through my first interviews as an embassy worker.

I began to learn the exact criteria the US embassy and immigration authorities were using to prioritize applicants for resettlement.

Yes, having a sponsor in the US was a plus, but it wouldn't help at all if you did not rank high enough on the priority list. Refugees were assigned a category based on their connection to the US, with the highest priority being for Category 1 "Refugees with close relatives (mother, father, sister, brother, or child) living in the United States." Category II was for refugees who were former employees of the US government in Indochina. Refugees who were closely associated with US policies or programs because of previously held positions in the former US-allied Indochinese governments or armed forces, or had been formerly employed by American firms or organizations, or who had trained in or been trained by the United States were Category III. The last and lowest priority were Category IV, refugees not accepted by a third country who should be granted parole on humanitarian grounds.

However, the US did not apply all the categories uniformly across all ethnic groups. The political situations in the different countries of origin were all unique, so the categories were adapted on a country-by-country basis, with the highest priority refugee population in Thailand being the Vietnamese, followed by the Lao. The Thai were eager to get the Vietnamese out of Thailand because of historical animosity, and the US felt a deeper obligation to the Vietnamese following the war and the subsequent US withdrawal. Therefore, in Songkhla, all categories were processed. But in the Cambodian case, with the Thai reluctance to allow US processing, the few refugees being processed for resettlement were limited to Categories I and II and only in select camps and in cases of special interest. It was now clear to me that as a Category IV, Thida was nowhere near being a priority.

I was struck by the contrasts between this population and the population in the Cambodian camps. While the Cambodian camps were filled with rural and minimally educated farmers, the Vietnamese refugees in the boat camps represented a greater cross section of society from the former regime. There were former government officials, actresses, teachers, artists and restaurateurs, cyclo drivers and factory workers. In that period, some high-ranking officers of the former Army of the Republic of Vietnam (ARVN, the defeated South Vietnamese forces) were being released after four- and five-year periods in "reeducation camps" and making their way onto boats leaving Vietnam. Songkhla was filled with former high-ranking members of the former South Vietnamese government and military.

With the assistance of the UNHCR and our very well-educated refugee interpreters, Larry and I interviewed refugees and prepared their files for presentation to US immigration officials, or Immigration and Naturalization Service (INS) officers.

The interviews were efficient, largely due to the efforts of our Vietnamese refugee workers who were all working well below their education and skill levels. One of my interpreters had been a translator at the Paris Peace Talks. Another interpreter, Le Thi Xinh, had been an exchange student in New Hampshire in the late sixties.

My main interpreter, Han Bin Quang, had been a journalist and had worked with Larry Burrows, a gifted photojournalist who had captured the inconceivable suffering of soldiers and civilians in the war on film. (Burrows himself would die in 1971 when the helicopter he and other journalists were in was shot down over Laos). Quang had served in the Army of the Republic of Vietnam and had worked closely with the Americans. He had even worked at the American embassy. General Westmoreland had personally presented a career longevity award to Quang for his service.

Quang had been to the US for training at Lackland Air Force Base in San Antonio in 1969, the year after the Tet offensive. His command of English was excellent, and he was well liked by everyone. But he was unable to escape in the chaos of the fall of Saigon in 1975, and he had been sent to reeducation camp under the new communist regime for nearly five years. On his release, he wasted no time finding his way onto a boat bound for Thailand. When we met, he was fifty—over thirty years my senior—and very much a man of the world. For some reason, he took a fatherly interest in me and would serve as both an interpreter and a guide to the Vietnamese people and their history and current plight, much like Ly had done in the Cambodian camp.

ACROSS A BRIDGE OF FIRE

For me, life in Songkhla was totally unlike life at the Cambodian border. I was safe, secure, and very comfortable. The duplex apartment where Larry and I resided was brand new and well furnished, with shining teakwood floors and clean, modern furniture. We had at our disposal a maid and a driver who taxied us about in a white, air-conditioned Toyota sedan. Songkhla was a peaceful, sleepy fishing town with a lovely beach. The camp was a quick ten-minute drive from our duplex.

Larry and I had a predictable routine. Early to rise, light breakfast, shuttled by car from our duplex to the little cramped and dirty camp ten minutes away. Eager, smiling Vietnamese interpreter staff efficiently arranged folding tables and metal stools, a nice cold glass of *café sio da*, sweet Vietnamese-style iced coffee, the interpreter's cigarette smoke. Friendly banter, a joke. The first family called. Eager. Nervous. Well-groomed in faded, ill-fitting camp clothes. Forms to be translated, statements to be signed. Family tree. Historical sketch. Thank you. Next family. Thirty, forty such a day. Metal tin boxes collecting the growing pile of files. Rubber stamps. The sound of yet another foreign tongue that was evocative, but elusive. The heat. The lazy breeze off the ocean. The excitement and urgency of the task. The boredom and tedium of the task. The white shirts and black pants and straw hats of the young Vietnamese women. Some very attractive. All unreachable to me, despite proximity. The last interview. The packing of the tin file boxes, the trek to the car. Back to town, and a leisurely evening. Perhaps dinner in the market, then more paperwork at home. Books from Larry's well-stocked library of Penguin classics. Letters home. The slow pace of life in Songkhla. The satisfaction of helping move people through a refugee camp to freedom in America.

Still, there was something awkward and uncomfortable about my position. The refugees, regardless of age or education or social status, treated me with great deference. Larry and I were the representatives of the US government, the ticket to freedom. I remember a Vietnamese physician and former officer who had survived reeducation camp sitting across from me at the interview table. I was in awe of him because I dreamed of becoming a doctor. He was nervous and overly eager to please. This didn't seem right. It seemed upside down and backwards.

I learned from the Vietnamese refugees that the war in Cambodia was going poorly from their perspective. The Vietnamese Army had invaded Cambodia and toppled the Khmer Rouge regime just over a year ago; that is what created the opportunity for the Cambodians to flood the Thai border seeking refuge. While the Vietnamese Army had installed a pro-Vietnamese government in Phnom Penh, the remnants of the Khmer Rouge and smaller non-communist resistance fighters continued to fight from their bases on the Thai-Cambodian border. In the most recent arrivals of Vietnamese boat refugees, the largest group were draft-aged men. As the war in Cambodia dragged on, the draft age had been lowered from eighteen to seventeen, and basic training cut form one year to six months—and in some cases only a few weeks. The Cambodia invading force was made up of Vietnamese regulars and *Khmer Khrom* (ethnic Cambodians from the former South Vietnam) draftees and other Cambodian refugee conscripts. In spite of being ousted from Phnom Penh, the Khmer Rouge continued to mount armed resistance from the border. The war ground on, and the young men arriving in our camp wanted no part of it.

As I worked in the Vietnamese camps, doing my duty, the thought of my Cambodian friends was never far from my mind. Talk of the war in Cambodia only served as a reminder. And headlines in the *Bangkok Post* announced that forced repatriations of Cambodians across the border back into a country still at war were imminent.

Dennis monitored my progress from Bangkok. He was impressed by my productivity. While Larry also seemed pleased with my work, he was easygoing and never put any pressure on me. In late July, Dennis informed me that on my eighteenth birthday, I would be hired as a full-time caseworker at full salary. I had earned it, he said.

I was filled with pride. Weeks ago, I was unemployed in a foreign country with an expiring visa. Now, I was about to become a full-time salaried US embassy caseworker.

Dennis believed in me. But with that faith came a self-imposed pressure to perform. The importance of moving people through the camp to freedom weighed upon me. Dennis reinforced the urgency of the work with telephone pep talks every evening. In his effort to praise and mentor me, I felt an overwhelming obligation to deliver.

In a letter home to my parents, I confessed to feelings of stress I would never share with Dennis or Larry. I did not want to look weak.

> *... I am genuinely happy here, and I haven't yet been significantly depressed. This is not to say that the pressure does not exist, for the pressure I face is more overwhelming than anything I've dealt with before. But I can withstand the pressures now. I have to. The pressures are such that if I start to give, my stability will crumble, like a dam with at first only a small crack.*

I had provided Ly with my address, and we corresponded regularly after I left Mairut Camp. Shortly after we parted, he wrote.

June 3rd, 1980

Hello my dear Good boy,

Everybody in Ly's house was sad since Scott left, especially your mother Kolap she was not o.k. Joan comes to see us today. She told me that you asked her to see us everyday. Did you? It makes Kolap feels a little better. She will go to the doctor in the Old Camp tomorrow.

O.K. Do you have any news from the Australian Embassy and U.S. Embassy for me? Please let me know. Sokhy bought a hen and a rooster last Sunday. Tim bought a bag for me, it cost 415 baht. It's a nice bag.

Thida ask me to give her greeting to you for her.
O.K. bye! bye! Take care of yourself.

Much love from your
Ly

June 13, 1980

Dear Scott,

Your letter arrives today. It's wonderful. Did you see my letter?
Kolap is o.k. now. Although she's to see the doctor but she's o.k. Bad news came from Saigon 2 days ago. My mother-in-law left my children for Laos. They have nobody to live with to take care of them. They said that they are lonely, cold, hungry- they missed us very much. They said that they will die of starvation because they will run out of money that I left very soon. Kolap is very sad when she heard this news. It's very hard for me a father stay and do nothing in the camp-prison while my children are calling for help. What can you help me do about this? Scott?

Your poor friend,
Ly

Thida wrote as well, but it was more difficult for her as she had to use someone to help her translate her letter into English.

June 21st, 1980

Dear Scott!

Well, my dear brother, for a month ago passed that you and I were separated, and I never have any news from you, so I try to write a letter to you, want to ask you about your health and your daily living.

What do you feel now? Are you well? Or Not? If you're so well, I, myself, will be very happy, and every day I am very well, have not anything bad in my daily life. But, especially, I think of you all the time. I miss our reminder that we have done together, *such as we all have had a delicious lunch, we often take for a walk on the beach, we have told the funny story or chatted together every day. So, nowaday, I have no anyones to talk with (in the funny story ways), have no anyone to ask and study with about English language. But, however, I will be trying to learn it by myself and I won't forget you until the end of my life.*

Write to me as soon as possible.

Thida

MOM AND DAD VISIT

As July approached, I looked forward to a much-needed break. My parents had rearranged their lives on relatively short notice and were coming to Thailand for a visit. Less than four months after I had left them, having never really considered a trip to Asia before, they embraced my mission and were eager to see a new part of the world. I had already secured some time off and planned to bring them to the border to meet my friends. The days passed slowly as I waited anxiously to be reunited with both my parents and my friends in Mairut.

I was excited that my parents were coming. So much had happened to me, and letters just didn't fill the void of conversation. Also, their visit was an excuse to get back to the border to see Ly, Kolap, and Thida and her family. I had used my connections to people still working in Mairut to secure proper border passes for myself and my parents—quite a feat.

Despite being a family visit, this was no tourist itinerary, and the ever-changing events on the border conspired to disrupt our plans. In late June, just weeks before my parents were to arrive, the Vietnamese launched a large offensive across the Thai border. While smaller incursions of Vietnamese troops in "hot pursuit" of Cambodian rebels were a daily occurrence, this was a significant one.

"Vietnam Forces Invade Thailand!" screamed the headlines in both the Bangkok and the international papers. Some 2,000 Vietnamese troops, backed by tanks and artillery, had come deep into Thai territory on the more crowded border camps well north of Mairut, overrunning three Thai villages and three refugee camps. Casualties in the camps were reported to be high. The Vietnamese had repelled a Thai counteroffensive, leaving 30 Thai soldiers dead, 150 wounded, and over 20 missing in action. Cambodian casualties were not yet known, but as the Cambodian rebel camps were the target of the offensive, they were feared to be high. Border hospitals were being overrun with casualties. The papers called the offensive the heaviest fighting since the Vietnamese first invaded Cambodia two years earlier.

While all this transpired, I was stuck hundreds of miles away, far from the front in the fishing village of Songkhla. I was glued to my shortwave radio around the clock, and I had an impulse to drop everything and head back to the border.

My colleague, Larry Crider, advised caution. If Larry had not advised me to lie low, I most surely would have impulsively taken off for the border.

"Sit tight," he told me, as we sat down to dinner after listening to the evening update on the BBC. "They wouldn't let you anywhere near the border, anyway. Not in the middle of the fighting."

"But what am I doing here? I can't just sit here and do nothing!"

Larry assured me that while this was indeed a sizable incursion, it would end soon.

"Vietnam does not want to launch a full invasion of Thailand. They don't want to restart the Vietnam War. Their interests are tactical. They are trying to deal a blow to the Cambodian rebels on the border—no more. Mark my words, this will be over real soon."

I listened to Larry. He was older and wiser.

After a week of heavy fighting, resulting in hundreds of dead and wounded, the Vietnamese withdrew. The fighting had continued for a week, but it never extended down the border. My friends in Mairut appeared to be relatively safe for the time being.

As things settled down, the prospects of my planned border visit with my parents became plausible again.

While I awaited my parents' arrival, I continued to focus on the daily routine of preparing refugee applicants for the eventual arrival of US immigration officers. Still, with the visit of my parents only weeks away, my thoughts strayed from my new life in Thailand back to the home and friends I had left behind. Maybe it was the anticipation of being reunited with my mom and dad, but I was beginning to miss home.

In the middle of July, I boarded a Thai Airways flight from Songkhla to Bangkok to greet my parents. When my mom and dad came to the international arrival area, somewhat fatigued from the long flight, we greeted each other with great excitement. It was wonderful to see them, and I was eager to share with them this new world I had discovered.

For the first time in my life, my parents now relied on me to help them around. Naturally, they were perfectly capable travelers, but given my familiarity with the country and my rudimentary but functional Thai language skills, I negotiated their way through a three-week stay in Thailand.

I secured the best airport limo available, something I would never have done for myself, and we headed off to the Viengthai Hotel, which had been recommended by Larry. Although the Viengthai was the nicest hotel I had seen since arriving in Thailand (after all, it had air conditioning and carpet), my parents saw it for what it was—a rather seedy, dark place, with a few too many couples consisting of older Western men and young Thai women. The next day, we moved to a more stately nearby hotel called the Royal that was quirky as well, but much more suitable to their tastes.

Within days of arrival, we set out for Trat, a six-hour journey by bus. When we arrived, I secured a room for my parents in the Trat Hotel. I had prepared them for the rudimentary living arrangements, including their rather unwelcome first encounter with the Asian squat toilets. I did not secure a room for myself, as I planned to take advantage of the short visit to stay with Ly, Kolap, and Thida in the camp.

The following day, we hitched a ride with my old COERR coworkers to Mairut. It was the rainy season and the entrance road to the camp was impassable because of mud. My parents and I had to kick off our shoes, roll up our pants, and wade through the thick sticky mud to reach Bamboo Camp where Ly, Kolap, and Thida still resided.

In Cambodian culture, great respect is given to parents. Accordingly, my friends welcomed my parents with great fanfare and genuine enthusiasm. Kolap, Thida, and Kanya had prepared a feast, working with only the barest supplies and ingredients, including the low-quality rice that was rationed to them. The women crafted the meal from meager cuts of meat and vegetables, purchased from the Thai merchants who sold heavily marked up produce from stalls along the fences. Despite these challenges, the meal was exceptional, a tribute to their efforts and talent.

In anticipation of their trip, I had informed my parents of the needs in the camp. They arrived with a variety of gifts, including highly prized American Levi's blue jeans, as well as books, candy, and perfume for Kolap and Thida. My mother also brought letters to the orphans in the unaccompanied minors section of the camp from her third-grade class back in Connecticut.

At great expense compared to her meager resources, Thida had commissioned a painting of Angkor Wat, which was skillfully done by one orphan in the unaccompanied minors center as a tribute to my parents.

After a brief three-day visit, my parents gave Ly, Kolap, and Thida their assurances that they would do whatever they could to help them come to the United States. This was no small solace to them. It was one thing having a teenager on your side. It was a much greater thing to have the support of his parents. Having met them face to face and seen their desperate situation firsthand, my parents were as taken by them as I had been.

As we parted, I reassured Ly and Thida that I would return at the earliest possible opportunity. I offered some cautious words of encouragement and promised that I would continue to press for their cases at the embassy.

The remainder of the visit with my parents was divided between Bangkok and a side trip to Songkhla to see the Vietnamese camp where I worked.

Immediately after leaving Mairut, we took a bus several hours north along the gulf and found ourselves in the tourist beach resort of Pattaya. It seemed surreal to sit in an Italian restaurant in a four-star air-conditioned hotel so soon after leaving the refugee camp. We were, after all, just a little further up on the same coast. But we were in a different world.

The three weeks flew by too quickly, and I hated to admit to myself that I was more than a little homesick when I saw them off at the airport in Songkhla on July 31, 1980, the day before my eighteenth birthday.

And then, entirely due to circumstances I had brought upon myself, I was alone again.

MINH VAN

Up this point, I had scrupulously avoided even the slightest romantic notion involving any refugee. From the time I first met Thida's daughters, despite their charm and beauty, they had been like sisters to me, not objects of romantic interest. The motivating force that had called me to do this refugee work was so pure that I suppressed the urges of my raging hormones.

I understood that there was a significant inequality of power between myself as an American refugee worker and refugee women, and that rendered any intimate entanglement off limits. And despite my inexperience in the ways of romance, I understood romantic entanglements were as likely to produce pain as comfort to the people I was trying to help.

And, yet…

I had just turned eighteen. I was single, and I was far from home. As time went on, I had grown increasingly isolated and lonely.

I had wasted no time in finding flirtatious relationships with several young Thai women I had come to know in the local villages outside the camps, women unencumbered by the complications of refugee status. There was Pi Mai, the beautiful daughter of a Trat restaurant owner who had costarred in a few Thai comedy films with better known Thai film stars. That relationship went as far as a few trips to the local movie theater to see the Chinese kung fu and Thai romantic movies on nights when I stayed in Trat, always chaperoned by her older sisters. Then there was Fong, an earnest and sweet young woman in the town of Songkhla who had been eager to make my acquaintance and who spent many Saturdays with me and her best friend on the public beach and in the coffee house she ran where I played guitar in exchange for beer and ice cream. But these relationships never amounted to more than flirtations.

Larry Crider, my senior colleague in Songkhla, had returned to the US for a home leave and for a time, I was the only embassy worker left in Songkhla, further exacerbating my feelings of isolation. One day in camp after lunch, I was catching a quick siesta nap on a hard bench in the raised wooden building where we conducted interviews. As I lay on my back, I became aware that someone was very close to me. I opened my eyes and looked up.

Surely, I must have died and gone to heaven.

A strikingly attractive Vietnamese woman was looking directly into my eyes. She smiled.

"I hope I didn't disturb you," she said.

"No… not… not at all," I sputtered as I struggled to sit up.

Minh Van was petite, with bright eyes and a sparkling smile. She was one of the Vietnamese refugee interpreters in the group that worked for the UNHCR in Songkhla. We had not yet officially met, but I certainly had noticed her. She had fair skin that contrasted with her short black hair.

"Quang tells me you sing and play the guitar. Do you?"

My pulse raced. I tried to stay cool. "Well, sure. Yes!"

"I am a singer too. Perhaps we could sing together someday. There will be a show in the camp this Saturday night. I will be singing. Will you come?"

That Saturday night, I was mesmerized as I watched her sing popular Vietnamese and French songs at the camp show. The audience loved her and cheered and applauded with gusto. She had a beautiful voice. As she charmed her compatriots, she charmed me. Within weeks, we had rehearsed a few American folk songs together, and we performed for the refugees at the weekly Saturday night shows.

I still knew I should resist my feelings of attraction to her. But Minh Van was a light in all the darkness. The mood in the camp betrayed the hardship and the worry of the inhabitants. The long grey barracks of Songkhla looked sullen and worn, weighed down by the troubles of the men, women, and children they housed, crowded together, anxiously awaiting an opportunity to leave to somewhere, anywhere, safer than here. Boats still were arriving on shore, unloading the weary, traumatized passengers who had survived multiple attacks by pirates on flimsy boats not meant for ocean journeys.

Amid all this darkness, a young woman with eyes so bright they broke through the weariness, with a smile so endearing that it lifted the spirit of almost everyone—men, women, all ages—who paused if ever so briefly to take her in when she passed. Poised, confident, with an excellent command of French and English in addition to her native Vietnamese. And on Saturday nights, she would stride on to the makeshift stage in the camp, masterfully draw the audience in, and sing sad Vietnamese love songs that would break the hearts of the seven thousand residents of the camp who all stood enchanted by her spell.

It was all a performance. We all knew what she had been through, where she was, the horror behind her, the precariousness of her life in the camp, the struggles that would lie ahead, but in those moments on stage when her voice rose, we all believed in her. We were drawn towards her light.

I was captivated by Minh Van from the first moment I opened my eyes and saw her smile. But by the time she walked off the stage that first night, I was in love with her.

Until I met her, I had numbed myself to all the suffering, trauma, and death in the Cambodian and Vietnamese camps. I had to be strong. I had to be the good soldier.

Minh Van made me feel momentarily carefree again. It may have been infatuation, but I loved how it felt. It was like Demerol. It was literally music. It made the pain go away, leaving me in a pleasant delirium.

I was flattered by Minh Van's attention, but she had not approached me by accident. For her and everyone else in that place, I was not seen as an American teenager. I represented the American embassy. I was a ticket out. Given my role, everybody wanted something from me. Everybody needed something from me.

Therefore, I was not at all surprised when, early into our budding friendship, she asked if I could check on the status of her case for resettlement in the US.

I called Dennis in Bangkok and asked him to check on her file. We were both surprised to learn that she had long ago been approved by US immigration with a Category I status: the highest priority for resettlement that usually meant departure directly to the United States within months. So why was she still in Songkhla? It did not make sense that she had remained in camp for so long after approval by US immigration officers.

Upon further researching with the UNHCR in camp, I learned the disturbing truth. She had been rescued from a ship that had been attacked by pirates, as the majority of ships had been. In another well-known piracy case of the time, the *Koh Krah*, or Khra Island case, refugee boats had been intercepted by Thai pirates, and many of the Vietnamese men were killed at sea. The women were kidnapped and brought to a remote island, Krah Island, where, as Dennis had described, they were repeatedly raped, girls as young as ten and women as old as seventy. Military aerial surveillance photos of the event documented dozens of small fishing vessels, each typically with crews of eight to ten, around the island at a time when there were less than twenty women being held there. The pirates of Krah Island had been apprehended and there was to be a trial. The prosecutors needed victims of pirates to testify about their crimes.

Minh Van told me that her boat had been attacked by pirates as well, but, she said, she was seasick and weak, and the pirates left her alone. But her boat had been flagged as a case of interest for legal cases being pursued against pirates. Minh Van had been held back in order to serve as a witness at a trial, but in the end, she was never called to testify. In fact, she was never even aware of why she had been held back. Her departure had been delayed while the UN and international legal proceedings against the captured pirates dragged on.

The knowledge of her further misfortune only fueled my concern for her. Consequently, I found her modest advances—calculated or not—impossible to rebuff. Like my Thai flirtations, the relationship remained totally innocent. We ate lunch together in one of the little makeshift Vietnamese noodle shops in the camp on the beach. We sang songs together, or I accompanied her on the guitar. She was a gifted singer with a sweet and engaging voice, especially on ballads. And we performed in front of the captive audience of seven thousand refugees at one of the professionally done shows that took place in the camp.

By the time of my inquiry about her status, the *Koh Krah* trials had already taken place, and the fact that she had not been moved to the US was simply a bureaucratic oversight. When I brought her case to the attention of Dennis, he was immediately able to place her on the next movement list out of the camp to a transit center, where she would then be allowed to depart Thailand to be with her family in California.

Although I had been used, I was happy to be used. While I realized her interest in me was calculated, I had fallen in love with her. I said nothing about my feelings to Minh Van, however, knowing that I could not share those thoughts until we met again on a more equal footing in the United States. She was worth waiting for. and wait for her I would.

I was beginning to feel something I hadn't really felt since I had been burned at age ten: hope. I felt hope for the future.

MORE UNNECESSARY RISKS

One Saturday in Songkhla, in the period where I was the sole embassy worker in town, I went down to take pictures of the fishing pier. I did not own a camera, but Dennis had given me permission to borrow the embassy camera for personal use off hours. At the docks, I asked to step aboard the boat of some Thai fishermen to get a better shot of the docks and shops along the water's edge. The rugged seafarers welcomed me on to the ship, and only moments later took great delight and fell to the deck laughing when, on pulling the camera away from my eyes, I realized that the boat had shoved off from the pier and was chugging out to sea.

The fishermen were all well developed and muscular from their manual work of hauling heavy fishing nets from the ocean. They wore black and blue wraparound fisherman pants, a loose, oversized set of trousers that was secured around the waist like a towel. They were shoeless and shirtless, with sun darkened skin. None spoke a word of English, and my Thai vocabulary was hardly up to the task of negotiating my safe return to shore.

But a smile goes a long way, and I played along. After a bit of small talk, I timidly asked when they might be going back to port. The captain laughed and said ten or twelve days. He explained they were deep-sea fishermen, and our trip would take us up towards Cambodia and Vietnam.

"Don't worry," he said. "We have plenty of food. Fresh fish from the sea."

With that, one of the fishermen came out from below deck with an enormous pot of rice, followed by four or five pans containing a variety of freshly cooked seafood. The crew invited me to join them, and we all squatted on the deck. The seafood was wonderful, the little I had. The ten or so crew members inhaled the meal within a matter of minutes, leaving me only scraps.

At that point, one of the more heavily tattooed men grabbed me by the arm. He led me below deck to "see the engines." The engines were impressive, large, and loud. But what he really wanted to show me was lined up against the side of the hold. There, mounted on a rack, were five M-16 rifles. He picked one up, beaming with pride, and held it before me.

"See. You are safe with us." That was when it occurred to me that in addition to reaping the bounty of the sea, they were probably pirates. During the period of the Vietnamese boat exodus, many Thai fishermen had taken up the pirating of the boat refugees as a sideline. The Vietnamese were unarmed and weakened and were often carrying their life's savings with them in gold and other valuables.

Was I on a pirate ship?

I returned to the deck, and having exhausted the limits of my conversational Thai, I sat down and watched as the crew threw out nets and pulled them neatly back onto the ship. After a few hours, which was enough time for me to start worrying about how I would explain my lengthy absence and abandonment of my post to the embassy (sorry, but I was kidnapped by pirates), I was relieved to see the boat head back into the port. As the crew let me off at the dock, they again all had a good laugh at my expense and told me that they were leaving for the ten-day trip the next morning. They asked if I would like to come. I respectfully declined, and we parted.

To date, my journey had found me in a border combat zone, on rumbling overnight open-air buses, and small seedy drug infested hotels, and in the company of governors, diplomats, a queen, former prisoners of war, victims of the killing fields, victimizers, assassins, and now pirates. I exercised no discrimination and obviously very little of what could be called good judgment. I took it all in as it came before me. No time to reflect.

It was inevitable that my lack of judgment and savvy would trip me up. Within a week of the pirate encounter, more trouble came.

Dennis called me in Songkhla from Bangkok one evening. Larry was still in the states on home leave, and he had been replaced by a military veteran who had spent a great deal of time in Vietnam, Russ[1]. Russ spoke Vietnamese fluently and, within the Songkhla Camp, had Vietnamese friends and acquaintances that dated back to his days during the war in Vietnam.

"Do you have a file on a refugee named Tran[2]?" Dennis asked.

"Um, let me see. Yes. I have it here in the cases approved by the INS," I replied.

"Approved? What do you mean approved? You shouldn't have a file at all because I have the file here in Bangkok. He was previously rejected by the INS. You're holding a duplicate file!"

As it turned out, Tran was a friend of Russ. Tran had allegedly been cooperative with the communists during the war. More recently, he allegedly cooperated with pirates who ransacked his boat while en route to Thailand from Vietnam. In an effort to save his own neck, he allegedly told the pirates just who among his fellow travelers was hiding gold. As a result of these allegations, US Immigration had rejected him when he came before them seeking asylum. Normally, that would have been the end of it. But he was a friend of Russ's, and Russ felt he, and others, had been handled unfairly by the US Immigration and Naturalization Service.

Unbeknownst to me, Russ had fraudulently created entirely new files for Tran and the others and then re-presented the clean files—free of all damning allegations—to a newly arrived US INS officer.

---

1 Not his real name
2 Not the actual name

ACROSS A BRIDGE OF FIRE

Without any of the incriminating evidence on their records, the cases were all approved for resettlement in the US.

Dennis immediately summoned Russ and me back to Bangkok on the next available flight. We barely had time to pack. I packed light, assuming that the Bangkok visit would be brief.

Back in the Bangkok office, Dennis took me aside and explained to me what had happened with the fraudulent creation and presentation of the files. He reassured me that he knew Russ had acted independently. But the crime was serious, and Russ was potentially facing federal charges.

Dennis seemed upset that I hadn't noticed what Russ had been up to. I reminded him that Russ was the senior staff member on our team, and I took orders from him, not the other way around. In any event, he had slid the entire scheme by me, and I hadn't caught it until Dennis called it to my attention. I reminded Dennis that the embassy had sent me directly to the field without an hour of formal orientation while the older caseworkers hired from the US were provided with training before they were deployed to the field. And while everyone else seemed to know that Tran was an unsavory character, no one had bothered to mention that fact to me.

The days that followed were unbearable and confusing to me. There was a series of closed-door meetings regarding this crisis that I was excluded from. Without providing any details, Dennis would reassure me that things would work out fine. "Just lie low."

I was not reassured.

I began to feel like Dennis was not being completely forthcoming. He tried to assure me that he was only shielding me from some messy negotiations that went on with officials as high as the ambassador. Still, for the first time, with my immaturity and inexperience, I began to question the depth of Dennis's loyalty. I began to suspect that I was going to be left out to dry by the time this all settled. Dennis had been good to me, but ultimately, his eye was on the mission. If I had to be cut loose so he could get his job done, I felt like he'd give me up in a heartbeat.

At the same time, there was the first movement of Cambodian

refugees off the perilous border to a newly constructed "processing center" in Chonburi several hours outside Bangkok. As I was at loose ends while the file switching scandal stewed, Dennis sent me out to join the team in Chonburi.

"You wanted to get back with the Khmer. Here is your opportunity. Now, go!" Dennis said as he temporarily transferred me to the Cambodian Section. In parting, I was given a stern warning not to fraternize with refugees like Russ had. Keep your nose clean, Dennis counseled, and you'll get through this.

With the rapid turnover of expatriate staff, the guy who had been in the country or in a camp for a few months became the senior field worker. When the embassy sent the first crew to Chonburi to process Cambodians, I was among them.

By great fortune, and with serendipitous timing, Ly and Kolap had been transferred to Chonburi right before I arrived. The Canadian embassy had placed them on a list of refugees to be interviewed for asylum. This was the lucky break they had yearned for. On my first break from interviewing at Chonburi, I wasted no time in tracking them down. We were thrilled to be reunited in a camp far from the border.

Having had interviewing experience in Songkhla, I was ahead of most of the rest of the Cambodian Section team, who had been busy doing paper-based prep work in Bangkok prior to the opening of Chonburi. And when new caseworkers came to the field, I was asked to train them, as Larry had trained me only months earlier. The fact that I spoke some Khmer—never mind that it was barely enough to sustain a brief and superficial conversation—enhanced my stature among the rest of the newly fielded team and helped overcome the now familiar skepticism engendered by my youthful appearance. I was also one of only two caseworkers who had actually been on the border, the other being our team leader, a young, charismatic, red-haired man named Karl.

As odd as it was, the processing of the very first Cambodian refugees in Chonburi was made a monotonous task by the sheer magnitude of cases that needed to be prepared in such a short period of time by a freshly fielded team. Potentially compelling personal stories of persecution and flight were abbreviated into three-line biographies: the so-called "Rice-Farmer-Rice-Farmer-Rice-Farmer" biographies. "Sihanouk Regime: Rice Farmer. Lon Nol Regime: Rice Farmer. Khmer Rouge: Rice Farmer. Vietnamese Invasion: Fled to border."

Still, the first large call out of Cambodian applicants for asylum was a significant breakthrough, and the monotony of the actual work was balanced by the sense of opportunity and urgency.

The embassy field teams in those days were typically made up of young staff, men and women in their twenties and thirties who liked the excitement and didn't mind the rudimentary communal living arrangements and the scarcity of simple amenities like hot water and air-conditioning. Jeff Sandel, then in his sixties, stood out. He was a tall, salt-and-pepper bearded man with glasses. Jeff also stood out in another significant way. He had actually lived in Cambodia before the Khmer Rouge took power and he spoke Khmer fluently.

Despite the weakness of my own command of the language, Jeff and I were the only caseworkers who spoke any Khmer. Jeff was delighted to encourage and coach me, and in the evenings back in town over cheap Thai Mekong whiskey, he would wistfully recall the old days under the Sihanouk regime of the sixties when he was attached to the embassy in Phnom Penh.

In the camp, work went forward. I interviewed Cambodians of interest to US immigration, while Ly helped the Canadian delegation with their interviews. On some days when the Canadians weren't in camp, Ly was able to sit in as my interpreter.

The Canadians offered Ly, Kolap, and Sokhy resettlement in Canada. After conferring with me, they accepted the offer. While they had preferred the idea of coming to the US to be near my family, I advised them not to pass up any firm offer. So, Ly and Kolap were on their way to Canada, and their freedom and safety were simply a matter of patience and time.

Thida, however, remained in limbo on the border in Mairut. While Canada had called out a very small number of refugees from Mairut, the US was still not processing anyone from the border camps. I received weekly letters from her, increasingly despondent. She worried she would be left behind.

In October, on a free weekend, I made what would be my final visit to Thida, although neither of us knew it at the time. I had not been able to get to Mairut for some weeks and getting there this time proved difficult. First, my main ally, Dang, was no longer in Mairut, having been transferred to Sakeo. Many other volunteers I had known had completed their standard six-week tours and returned to the US and other countries. Fortunately, my friend Lucy Murphy of CONCERN was still there, and I hitched a ride into camp with my Irish friends. I had no official authorization to be on the border, and this time I would not dare to try and stay after dark. I banked on the hope that the soldiers would recognize the CONCERN van and not check passes. I got lucky. We breezed right past the perimeter gate with a casual hand wave of the sentry.

I was struck by the changes. Bamboo Camp had grown—it had tripled in population. The camp where Thida lived that only months earlier had been referred to as "the new camp" was showing signs of use and wear. It was dirtier, and the hastily constructed bamboo structures were graying and sagging. The sky was gray, the buildings were gray, the sand was gray—everything was gray.

Thida had no way of knowing I was coming, and I feared by that time she might have thought I would never come again. When I arrived at Building 19, no one from her family was there. Where had they gone? Had I lost them? I felt my heart start to race. A friend of Thida's recognized me.

"Where is Thida? The children?" I asked.

The children were in school and Thida was working with the Irish CONCERN agency. Thida's friend took me by the hand and led me towards the place in the newer part of the camp where Thida worked. A neighbor's children had run ahead to let Thida know I was there and as I approached her work area, Thida came running towards me.

I was struck by the look on her face. Before she saw me, there was fear and desperation and, at the same time, excited anticipation.

Then, as she spotted me and made eye contact, a smile, and a rush of overwhelming relief. She ran to me and grabbed my hands and held them tightly.

"Scott!" she shouted with her strong Cambodian accent. She held my hands even tighter.

She started talking in Cambodian, much too fast for me to comprehend half of what she was saying. Where had I been? How was I? Why hadn't I been back in so long?

As we approached her building, she shouted out to the children. "Come! Quickly! Scott is here! He came back! I knew he would come back!"

We talked of the uncertainty of her application for asylum. I gave her assurances that I would remain in touch with the embassy staff overseeing her case. Although she made every effort to smile and joke as she had before, this time, things were different. The initial euphoria of surviving the Khmer Rouge and Vietnamese and the dangerous border crossing had faded. She was worried, and she did not hide it.

Kanya and Chanthy seemed happy to see me, but Kanya, as usual, kept her distance. Chanthy was eager to demonstrate her newly acquired English language skills with me, and I was quite taken with her successes in such a short time.

I told Thida that Lucy Murphy had agreed to look out for her while she was in camp. I then discovered that Lucy had given her the job at CONCERN.

When I left, I promised to return as soon as I could. Each departure had become more difficult. This one somehow seemed particularly sad. Thida had been in Mairut Camp too long. Others had come and gone. We were all getting discouraged, although I could not show my sense of worry to her. It was increasingly obvious that she had no qualifications on which to construct a compelling claim for asylum in the US program, given the strict requirements.

As we said goodbye, Thida flashed her usual smile. Hopeful, but full of awareness that things might go poorly.

"Scott. When can you come again?" she asked in Khmer.

"I'll come back as soon as I can," I answered.

As I rode away from camp, dust trailing the van on the bumpy dirt road, I could not get the image of Thida's face out of my mind—her face when she first greeted me. It was so full of fear and relief at the same time. Sometimes, when you look into someone's eyes, you see too much. These were the eyes of a woman who had placed her complete faith in me. Who needed me. There was no turning back from that. While I knew I could not bear to leave her behind in that camp, I could not stay.

I wasn't even supposed to be there.

OVER MY HEAD

The entire time I worked with the embassy, I had mixed feelings about being paid to do refugee work. Until then, I had been a volunteer. At the embassy, I had a salary of $15,000 a year with housing allowance and redundant *per diem* compensation for all the time I spent upcountry. This was more than my mother, a public school teacher in Connecticut, was earning. Dennis addressed my guilt about being paid. "You are not taking money away from the refugees. It's US government money—and you are being paid a fraction of what they traditionally pay a foreign service officer to do the same work."

Still, I felt like the arrangement was morally deficient. This perception was compounded by the fact that the embassy, along with UNHCR, had the reputation among the "real" volunteers in the non-governmental voluntary agencies ("volags") of being fat and spoiled. As embassy staff, we rode in new air-conditioned vans or cars; the small volag troops more often were found in the bench seat backs of open-air pickups. The embassy folks had nice accommodations; the volag folks stayed in local homes or in rudimentary hotels or bungalows in the town near camp. And finally, the volag folks answered only to their agency hierarchy and sense of mission. The embassy was neck-deep in international diplomatic bullshit and was often hesitant in committing to anything in the way of assistance for individual refugees or families lest it be misconstrued as a "policy change" or set precedent. In spite of my pride at being an embassy employee, I felt morally corrupted by the cash. The pure volunteerism and freedom of my early months was gone. I had sold out. At least that's how I felt.

The money did allow me to help Ly and Thida in a more concrete and meaningful way, and it was during that time that I was first able to send them much needed money. I sent medicines and money to their children in Vietnam. Still, it added to my sense of corrupted ideals at a time when my whirlwind journey to Thailand had blown me off course from my initially pure and simple mission. On the border, things had been straightforward. Now, in the fast-moving and complex world of embassy work, things were rapidly getting complicated, and the more I knew, the less I understood about how to keep my own head above water, let alone help others.

On my return to Bangkok, I was summoned by Dennis. He called me into the back office he shared with Ed Powers, a charismatic redheaded Vietnam vet from Maine who had befriended and nurtured me along with Dennis in my brief time in the section. The office was a converted solarium surrounded by tropical greenery off the back of the townhouses on Wireless Road that served as the US Embassy Refugee Section. I sat down facing Dennis, who was behind his desk. Ed and Hien, the Vietnamese Section secretary, worked quietly at their desks to my left.

Dennis spoke in a controlled, flat tone. The file switching affair had been settled. INS would drop charges if Russ resigned and left the country...and if I would never be allowed to return to Songkhla again.

Wait. But I was innocent. I hadn't done anything wrong. So why was I being punished?

Inside, I felt my indignation welling up. To me, this settlement seemed to imply guilt on my part. I felt the implication of my complicity was unfair. My budding professional reputation I had strived so hard to establish was crumbling around me.

I looked directly at Dennis, and I knew I couldn't trust him. I struggled to remain cool. My voice was shaky, and then it involuntarily dropped to almost a whisper.

"Why...why didn't you defend me?"

The natural inference any reasonable person would draw, I said, was that I was being banned from working in Songkhla because I had some role in the scandal—that I had done something wrong.

Dennis became defensive and his tone turned paternalistic. "I defended you the best I could given a crappy situation. There are many things you are too young to understand. The charges are very serious. Laws have been broken. You're lucky to still have a job. You should be thanking me."

I felt betrayed.

"Dennis," I quaked. My hands were trembling. "You haven't been honest with me through this whole fucking thing."

For a moment, everyone in the room froze.

Dennis looked up at me. I had crossed a line in crudely challenging Dennis's integrity, especially in front of Hien. He shook his head. He drew a deep breath.

"That's it," he said. "You're fired."

I waited, just for a moment, for him to qualify his words, or retract them. I was stunned. I looked over at Ed for help. Ed looked awkwardly at the floor and said nothing. Hien remained poised and unflappable and continued to work quietly at her desk as if nothing had happened.

Finally, the weight and cumulative stress of my odyssey came crashing down on me all in that one moment. The fantasy of the adult me collapsed. I was just a dumb kid. The dumb kid who had lit himself on fire.

I rose from my chair in a daze. I lingered awkwardly for a moment, and, feeling dizzy, stumbled out of the office. No one stopped me. No one came after me.

Almost to the front door of the Refugee Section, I bumped into my friend Larry Crider, who was just returning from his six-week home visit to the US. He had missed the entire Russ incident and naturally, he was completely oblivious to the exchange that had just transpired between me and Dennis. He smiled. "Scott! How are you?" Then he saw my face.

"What's wrong?"

I didn't know what to say.

"I'm... I'm going home," I said. Before I could suppress them, tears filled my eyes. Tears. For the first time since I had arrived in Thailand. Possibly for the first time since I had left the hospital eight years earlier. I had been holding a whole lot in for too long.

Overwhelmed and embarrassed, I pushed past Larry and bolted out into the brightness and smothering heat of the Bangkok midday sun.

THE BOTTOM

I had failed.

Thida was still on the border, and I had just blown my best chance to help her by getting myself fired. She had believed in me, and I had not delivered.

I had failed Dennis, who also had believed in me, who had given me a chance.

I spent the weekend adrift, wandering aimlessly around the streets and *sois*, strolling down the small side streets and shops, riding circular routes through the hot, hazy, smoggy streets of Bangkok on the open-air buses, staring at the wall in the Bangkok apartment I had rented near Dennis, feeling sorry for myself. I finally went to see Ed Powers. I had no idea what to do next and I needed someone to talk to.

"Hey, stranger. How are things?" Ed greeted me at the door of his apartment and put his arm around my shoulder.

"You tell me," was the only thing I could think to say.

"Have you talked to Dennis?" he asked.

"Ed, you were there. He fired me. He was furious. Of course I haven't talked to him."

"Well," Ed continued in a reassuring tone, "I have talked to him, and I know he's really upset about what happened. He's not really happy about how that all went down. I think you should go see him. You two need to talk. He actually thinks the world of you."

To me, Ed was genuine. As with Dennis, I looked up to him, but in a different way. Ed was a straightforward guy who eight years earlier had tiptoed throughout the minefield of his own tour in Vietnam. Ed was a survivor. Ed was a role model. He was one of the quickest wits I had ever met. I observed carefully as he skillfully deployed humor and wit to deflect stress, and maybe to obscure pain. He was kind to me, even if he had left me hanging only days before in my confrontation with Dennis—though I'm not sure how he could have handled the situation differently.

Ed was the type of friend I needed very much at that given moment. I trusted his judgment. Based on his advice, I went to see Dennis.

Dennis lived only two doors away from my apartment. This was no accident. Dennis had helped me find this little studio apartment when I started to feel like I had overstayed my welcome by continuing to stay with him and his family on my weekends in Bangkok.

I walked the short distance from my apartment to Dennis's house on the corner of the *soi*. I rang the gate buzzer and was greeted by his maid, who recognized me and invited me in. Dennis came to the door of the house to meet me. "Come on in." There was no malice in his voice. He sounded tired.

We sat down. We talked. I apologized for having lost my composure, for having cursed at him. Dennis expressed his regret that he had responded reflexively, and he apologized for firing me. He said he had been disappointed because he had misjudged me. I had carried myself so well, he explained, performed so well on the job, interacted so well with coworkers twice and three times my age, moved in and out of cross-cultural circumstances so well, he assumed I was more mature than I really was. I confided that maybe we both had wrongly assumed that.

We had a good talk, and I felt a tremendous sense of relief. I needed Dennis's approval, his support. I needed him to believe in me again.

ACROSS A BRIDGE OF FIRE

I had thought he would never speak to me again, or, if he did, the friendship would be over. It was not. He clearly still cared about me.

He casually mentioned that he had rescinded my termination, but as we talked more, I began to wonder if my separation from the embassy might actually be for the best. I had reached my limit. For the first time, I was ready to admit that I was far away from home and in way, way over my head.

Dennis gave me a pep talk. I had stumbled but not fallen. He convinced me to return to work. But he warned me that although he had done his best to clear my name from any association with the file manipulation in Songkhla, the issue of my unauthorized visits to the border was causing heartburn at the State Department level of the agency. My visits to Mairut had been reported up the Thai military chain (flashing that embassy I.D. had done me in). He was not sure how that was going to turn out. "Unless you're a spook, you have no business on that border. It sends the wrong message to the Cambodians. The embassy Refugee Section *in particular* has no permission to be on that border."

Despite our rapprochement, I sensed that the end was near. I felt like the walls were closing in on me.

I was exhausted. I had done my best to stand up straight, to be an adult, to be a good soldier. But I was spent. I just wanted to collapse into a ball on the floor. I was resilient and I was strong, but I had my limits—and I had exceeded them.

In coming days, I continued to talk with Dennis and Ed about my situation and my overall emotional state. In the course of those conversations, I came to the humbling conclusion that it was time for me to go home.

I was emotionally depleted, and I felt like I could no longer muster the energy to continue playing the part I had been playing. This unlikely house of cards of my fledgling international career as a teenage refugee worker was collapsing around me. I had only been in Thailand for eight months, but it seemed like a lifetime.

I agreed to finish out the month, as I did not want to miss the historic opportunity to process some of the first Cambodian cases out of Chonburi. I would then resign my embassy position and return to the United States.

Later that week, I went up to the office of Bill Sage, then the Joint Voluntary Agency representative, the director of the refugee program. As I had spent all my time in the field, I had never been near his office. His secretary asked who I was.

"Scott Allen."

From an open door, Bill, who I had barely met, looked up.

"Oh, Scott. Yes. If you have a moment, uh, I need to talk with you."

He shifted awkwardly in his chair as I stepped into his office. He fumbled for words as he tapped his pen on the glass top of his large wooden desk.

"Scott, I need to ask you, were you aware of the fact that there is a strictly enforced policy forbidding anyone associated with the United States embassy, and particularly the Refugee Section, from visiting the border camps?"

"Yes, I was aware," I responded. I could tell where this was going.

"You also understand violation of this policy would result in immediate termination from this agency?" he continued, his eyes shifting nervously.

"Mr. Sage, before you continue, perhaps you should read this letter. I came here to deliver this to you." I could have let him continue, but the thought of hearing the words, "you're fired" for the second time within the same week was more than I could bear.

He opened the letter I had been holding in my hand. I had just typed it on embassy letterhead. The subject line read *One Flew Over the Cuckoo's Nest*.

Bill read the memo. It was my letter of resignation. He raised his eyebrows, then leaned back in his chair. He raised his eyebrows again. "Well. Hmm. I see," he muttered. "Well, I guess that's that."

He stood and came around the desk to shake my hand. "Listen, I want to thank you for your service." He gave me a firm, businessman's handshake.

I shook his hand, turned, and walked out the door.

29

LOOSE ENDS

When I had been summoned to Bangkok from Songkhla, I had left most of my belongings, including a newly purchased guitar, behind. As I was not allowed to return to Songkhla, Dennis arranged for my things to be brought to Bangkok on a bus transfer of refugees accepted for resettlement in the US. The refugees would travel for eighteen hours from southern Thailand to reach the transit center outside the capital. They would have my things on the bus.

As luck would have it, Minh Van was on that bus, and she kindly agreed to carry my things. I would travel to the Rangsit Transit Camp on the outskirts of Bangkok to meet her and the others to collect my things.

One evening after work, I took the city bus along the route Dennis instructed and was surprised when I arrived and first laid eyes on Rangsit Transit Camp as night was falling. It looked nothing like any of the refugee camps I had seen before. It was a sparely appointed urban concrete landscape, dark and lit only by a few spotlights and naked bulbs attached to precariously strung electrical wires that ran from building to building. The housing was the uncompleted shells of three- and four-story shop houses. The whole thing was more like a scene from a post-apocalyptic movie than a refugee camp, and as I entered the compound, I was briefly disoriented by the glare of the spotlight in my direction.

One of my former interpreters from Songkhla recognized me and called out. He led me to where Minh Van was temporarily quartered. She smiled and immediately began thanking me profusely for helping her get on the transfer list. She was going to America!

She and the others asked me to take out my guitar that Minh Van had brought to me, and I played as Minh Van sang a mournful Vietnamese ballad, followed by "Leaving on a Jet Plane."

"When I get to America, will I see you there?"

"Well, you are going to California, and I live on the East Coast. It's very far from where I live. But I will find a way to come see you."

It was one small, but important victory. Minh Van was getting out of here. I still held out hope for some kind of a future between us, but that would still have to wait. At least she would finally be safe. For now, that was enough.

I WAS RUNNING OUT OF OPTIONS for Thida. I had damaged my own credibility and much of my influence at the embassy. I was soon to be unemployed, and despite my very brief tenure as a salaried employee, I was nearly broke. I was running out of time, and there was now no way I would be permitted anywhere near the border under any circumstances. But I knew of one person in the Khmer Section who might be able to help. Jeff Sandel, the Khmer speaker who I had worked with in Chonburi, had also worked with the embassy in Cambodia before the fall of Phnom Penh.

I had told Jeff about Thida early on. I knew I needed his support. He appreciated my attachment to and affection for Thida and her children, and he agreed to work with me on finding an angle to raise her priority. As it was, she was just another name on a master list of over two hundred thousand, at a time when the number of Khmer being accepted for resettlement was only two or three thousand, roughly one in a hundred. It was a daunting task, but Jeff was supportive.

After reviewing her story again with me, as well as I knew it, he seized on Thida's deceased husband. "What did you say her husband did?"

"She says he was a teacher and later a director of a school in Battambang."

"The director of a school. And that school would likely have been government run. Get me the name of that school if you can. If it was a government school, and he served in that capacity under the Lon Nol regime, she would move from a Category E (no-claim) to a category D (association with the former US-backed government). That would at least qualify her for inclusion on an interview list. If we can get her in the game, I can take it from there."

On one of my last visits to Mairut, I had clarified the details: her husband had been director of the high school at Thmar Puok; indeed, a government position. I relayed this information back to Jeff.

Earlier in the week that ended with the confrontation in Dennis's office, Jeff sent me a note through interdepartmental mail. It was a note with several different scripts from different writers. It had begun as a note from Jeff to Cynthia in the Cambodian Section.

Phanat Nikhom. Chonburi
13 OCT 80

Cynthia:

There's a case in the bamboo camp, Mairut (2000) which I think merits our consideration for call-out. It is T-313082: DUONG THIDA (8). She shows a CAT E in the master list, but in fact she is a strong CAT D. (Her husband was a high school teacher and was killed by the Red Khmer.)

I think her category should be changed and that she should be called out at the earliest opportunity.

Thanks,
Uncle Jeff

P.S. The information on the P.A.'s husband is not in file. It was gathered on the ground in Mairut.

Then, in Cynthia's green pen:

Jeff—looks like CB VI okay—

"CB VI" or Chonburi VI, was an embassy callout list to be submitted to the Thais via the United Nations high commissioner for refugees, requesting movement of listed refugees from the border to the processing center of Chonburi. Then, in yet a third unidentified hand, the word:

DONE

Jeff had then folded over the note and addressed it to me with the following salutation:

*Scott—
Looks like we won this one.
Regards,
Jeff*

I was not able to see Thida again before I left. The border was clearly off limits to me now. I did not have the opportunity to say good-bye to her.

I would have preferred to have stayed until Thida left the country, but realistically I knew that could be another six to twelve months. At least she was on the next "call list" of refugees in Mairut to be interviewed by the US, whenever that callout could be negotiated and authorized. That gave me limited reassurance. Even in my current situation, I could not have left Thailand with anything less.

COMING HOME AGAIN

On October 28, 1980, I stepped past the embarkation desk of Thai immigration and boarded a 747 on a flight that would return me to the United States via Hong Kong. When the plane touched down in New York, I was as excited as I had been when I touched down in Thailand eight months earlier.

At the terminal, my parents and my grandparents greeted me with hugs and smiles. I remember talking nonstop the entire two-and-a-half-hour ride from New York to Connecticut in an excited jet-lagged effort to share all the dramatic events that had transpired.

We arrived home after midnight. I was so worked up and agitated that I couldn't sleep. My parents went to bed, as they would have to work the next day. My sisters, now fifteen and eleven, were already long asleep. I sat alone in my basement bedroom that looked just as it had the day I left, thinking about the other universe I had discovered, thinking of Ly and Kolap...and of Thida and her children who I had left behind. I thought of Minh Van. Maybe she was already in California. I was jet-lagged and overstimulated. I began to wonder if the whole thing had been just a dream.

At six o'clock the next morning, I crashed and slept for twenty-four hours straight.

IN A CONVERSATION my father and I had during his visit to Thailand, he predicted that after all this worldly freedom and adventure, coming home was going to be a letdown. Like coming down off a high. Like when the Demerol wore off. I would now see his prophecy come to pass.

Bates College had graciously agreed to let me start with the January semester, even though I had requested and been granted a deferred admission for the following year. I gratefully accepted the offer as my bargaining position with other colleges was nonexistent. That left me with two months to fill, and I reluctantly returned to work for the Mintz and Hoke advertising agency I had been employed at during my senior work-study. The job that had once seemed so cutting edge now seemed ordinary and unimportant.

Of course, I had something of a hero's welcome in my town. When I visited my old high school, teachers and students alike came running up, giving me hugs and praise. But hero's welcomes are brief and fleeting, and in no time, I was just another kid working as an errand boy for a local business.

That November was made more depressing for me with the assassination of John Lennon and the election defeat of Jimmy Carter. Lennon and the Beatles had, of course, been my childhood heroes and the source of immeasurable comfort. As a young adult, the thoughtful and peace-oriented Carter represented decency and respect for human rights. While he was blamed for the failed Iran hostage rescue mission, I had come to know him through his policies and practices in the refugee program. His humanistic approach offered more hope for a more favorable interpretation of asylum application by refugees still on the border—a quality that was very important to me and my new friends, but apparently not high on the list of the electorate at large. With the Carter defeat and the Lennon assassination, I felt thoroughly disenfranchised in a country where I now felt like an outsider.

While I was still in Thailand, my mom had followed my lead in becoming totally engaged in supporting Southeast Asian refugees. Her third-grade students wrote letters to the orphanage in Mairut, and while we waited for Thida, she befriended and supported a Cambodian family and a Vietnamese family who had just arrived locally in northwestern Connecticut. In time, her commitment and involvement with these families struggling to adjust to life in Connecticut put my efforts to help refugees to shame. She and my dad would help them secure donated or cheap furniture for their new apartments, help them learn where to shop, how to set up accounts with the utility companies and open a bank account. They would be available for advice and guidance as newly arrived refugees adapted to life in this new world, much as Ly had helped me understand my new world when I arrived in Mairut. The refugee families she helped grew to treasure the friendship and support of both my parents, and in turn, my parents were delighted to explore their new relationships with these new Americans and learn about their cultures. Meeting her new friends helped fill the gap, but I was still fixated on Thida.

I now had no good way to communicate with Thida other than the mail, which was slow and unreliable, with some letters taking two months to reach their destination and some not reaching it at all. Although I had managed to get her on the embassy interview list, I could not escape the fact that I had left the border before she had. I was in the US. She was still at risk of being forcibly returned to Cambodia. And not only Thida, but her children too. The thought of all of them stuck on the border continued to haunt me. In December, having not heard anything reassuring about their status, I wrote again to Jeff Sandel in Bangkok.

Over the winter holidays, my parents and I continued to receive a steady stream of letters from an increasingly distressed Thida. Naturally, I responded to every letter, each one assuring her that I was continuing to do what I could from the United States.

In one of her earlier letters to my parents, written while I was still in Thailand, Thida told my parents that I had visited her and slept in camp one night, a visit that, in her words, "seemed to reduce my trouble." She voiced growing concern for her safety and said she feared for her future. She wrote with restrained sorrow about the departure of Ly and Kolap, as well as other lucky residents of Mairut who had also been accepted for resettlement.

Thida's letters were crudely written in broken English, but her despair as well as her strength came through to me as if I were still sitting next to her on the floor of Building 19 in Mairut Camp, holding her hand and feeling the warmth and comfort of her friendship. I could not help but wonder if I would ever hold that hand again, the hand that had first reached out to me in her bold effort to secure my attention eight months earlier on the Cambodian border.

IN JANUARY 1981, I arrived on the campus of Bates College in Lewiston, Maine. I was ready to begin a new stage in my life. I was eager to fill in tremendous gaps and voids of knowledge concerning the world I lived in. I was ready to learn.

But, in my first months at Bates, I underwent a process of reverse culture shock not unlike the reentry period I had experienced after being discharged from a Boston burn center to a quiet suburban fifth-grade class eight years earlier. Having just returned from the world of refugee work in a third-world combat zone, here I was, on a quiet remote Maine campus, with twelve hundred or so students mostly from small New England towns like my own. As with my return from the burn ward, I quickly realized I had no one to talk to who shared my experience or perspectives—or, at least, none that I could easily identify.

In orientation with the few other so-called "January freshmen," I was approached by Cedric Sherman, a friendly and outgoing student from New Jersey who had whiled away the first semester on his own adventure, hitchhiking through Europe. We were each relieved to find someone who wanted to talk about the world beyond the small universe of Bates, and we immediately hit it off. Together, we eventually befriended Roget, a student from Cameroon, with an interest in international diplomacy.

The three of us would chew up hours of after-dinner time

debating and arguing about international news and politics. We would scour the AP ticker in the lobby of Chase Hall for a scoop or a news bulletin on something related to a country of our interest. And, during our discussions, they learned the story of Ly, Kolap, Thida, Quang, and Minh Van.

I took comfort in their friendship.

Shortly after I arrived at Bates, I started receiving, a month or so after they had been written, more desperate letters from Thida, then still in Mairut, on the border right where I had left her. She was stranded and very much at risk, and the magic that had made me appear to be powerful and influential when I was an embassy worker had vanished. The spell was broken. I was back to being what I really was. Just another college kid with very little power, no money, and no influence.

In December, I received a letter from Thida. Thida could not speak English, or write it for that matter, but enterprising refugees with some language proficiency would translate letters for a fee. While the exact words were those of an anonymous refugee translator, her voice came through to me as I read.

Mairut
December 25, 1980

Dear Scott

Along time ago that you have left me. Until now, I always think of you and your family very much. Whenever I never get your letter which make me to hear about you and your family. Though I see and live with you in a short time, I still like you and love you like my family. Now How are you today? And how is your family? Every day, are you at university or not yet?

Now I am very sad that I hear they said: They will send Khmer refugee back to Cambodia. This bad news I have heard from the foreigner who comes from the meeting at Bangkok. Is that true or not? If I return to Cambodia, I will be difficult to live because I have no house no relative especially my parents who I know whether they are alive or not? The important this is rice that I have no money to buy it for all my children. I think I won't be able to meet you in the future and I want you to help my family as soon as possible because you already know about five years ago under Pol Pot so we dislike the communists regime we won't go back to meet them again.

In the end of my letter, I wish you and your family happy all the time. With the highest hope. God bless you in news year. With thanks and hope from,

Mother-in-law
Thida Duong

As I considered my limited options, I thought about leaving school again and returning to Thailand. I should never have left with Thida still on the border. I sought the advice of my parents.

Although they understood my concern for Thida, they seemed not to fully understand how the task of helping Thida was important and everything else was not. For good reason, they began to worry I might do something stupid again, and the telephone calls that were meant for support often took a turn towards parental admonishment to "stay focused" and not to "get too distracted." Telephone conversations were followed by letters bearing the same supportive parental advice. I did not doubt their love, and I knew they were trying to understand. But we were living completely different lives. How could they possibly understand?

On the other hand, I did know someone who might. My father's father, Grampi, was a combat veteran who had volunteered for the navy at age thirty-nine with a wife and three small children that he would have to leave behind, and had served in the South Pacific for three years of the second world war. He was a taciturn man, stoic, and not easily excited. In his gentle, caring, working man's way, he carried his own burdens of surviving the war with grace and dignity when I knew him as an older man.

Grampi and I had never discussed his war experience except once, briefly, back in 1972 while I was undergoing care for my burns at the Shriner's Burn Institute in Boston when he gave me the wooden plaque with the insignia of his squadron. I felt like Grampi might understand the things I was wrestling with. He had returned from war and reentered society.

Like my relationship with Ly, Kolap, Thida, and Kanya, Grampi and I had that unspoken connection that took root during his visits to the Shriner's. I don't begin to compare my experience on the Cambodian border with three years on a PT boat in the South Pacific during the war any more than I do my burn traumas to the suffering of the Cambodian refugees. But there was something about Grampi that was on the same wavelength as my Cambodian friends. I felt like I did not need to explain certain things. He seemed to understand the most important parts before I even spoke.

I called him from Bates—he lived less than an hour away in York, Maine.

"I've been having a difficult time getting back into things here. I keep thinking about the people I left behind."

"Alright," he replied. "Dorothy and I are coming up."

With that, he and Dorothy, his second wife, drove up to see me. Within an hour, he pulled up to the front of my dormitory, where I was waiting.

Grampi had been an auto mechanic and he loved to drive. We did not need a destination. He just drove around the narrow streets with worn and weathered tri-decker homes in the working-class neighborhoods of Lewiston while I talked.

He listened while I rambled on about my experiences. I said I felt even more out of place than before I left. Returning to America seemed harder than the culture shock I had experienced when I arrived in Thailand. I felt guilty for leaving everyone behind, especially Thida's family—and for that matter, the thousands of others who continued to languish and suffer while I enjoyed the peace and security and opportunity afforded me as an American college student.

He listened quietly and patiently, but I sensed something I said was connecting with him.

Grampi pulled the car over to the side of the road. He looked over at me and nodded his head in understanding. Then he looked out the front window. And then for the first time, he spoke openly to me about the war.

"I think I understand why you went to Thailand. When the Japanese attacked Pearl Harbor, I knew enlisting was the right thing to do. You felt helping those refugees was the right thing to do. I know how that feels. You couldn't *not* do it."

He told me about training with the young recruits, half his age, who laughed and joked as they shot targets in training exercises off the coast of California. He recalled their youthful smiles as they left the West Coast, bound for Australia. Those smiles were gone after the first encounter with the Japanese, when he and his crew pulled the wounded survivors of another sunken PT from the water. He accompanied another badly wounded soldier from his boat to the hospital on a supporting battleship and sat with a young navy doctor at the boy's bedside as he died, admiring the doctor's determination to save his patient even though they both understood it was a futile effort. In the years that followed, he would bury more young men at sea.

After three years in the South Pacific, the constant fear and loss and unending stress ground away at him. He became disillusioned with the military and its leaders. In his view, the Americans had suffered excess casualties in an ill-conceived holding pattern off occupied Australian islands, an effort that was undertaken merely to allow time for the Australian Forces to retake islands from the Japanese themselves for reasons of national pride. His squadron then suffered heavy losses in two friendly fire incidents. He saw the rampant waste and destruction and lack of coordination that reigned in the storming of Red Beach and the retaking of Leyte in the Philippines. After three and a half years without a break or a home leave, the atomic bombs were dropped, and the war was over. But he was not released from service. He was a mechanic, and the navy wanted him to stay in theatre as they decommissioned PT boats in the Philippines. After repeated requests for a home leave were rebuffed, he boarded a US-bound ship and headed home himself, without orders or approval.

This part of the story I had never heard before. My grandfather, the war hero, had gone AWOL. Well, I thought, that's an Allen for you. He volunteered to do the right thing, but on his own terms. And when he was done, he was done.

He came home—to an ungrateful nation. After three and a half years of service as a warrant officer in command of a PT boat squadron that suffered among the highest casualties of any squadron, the navy gave him a demotion in rank and a dishonorable discharge for abandoning his post—after the war was over. With the encouragement and support of his congressman, he went to the Pentagon in Washington, D.C. to explain his actions. There he succeeded in securing a satisfactory discharge—less than the honorable discharge which he wanted and deserved, but certainly preferable to a dishonorable discharge.

Like me, he had found returning harder than going. He, too, was overcome with guilt for having survived when young men did not. Having left with the highest faith in his government, he had become disillusioned with it. When he saw how politics took precedence over human life, he felt betrayed.

For years, he was angry and irritable, and he admitted that it probably affected his relationships with his wife and children. Grampi did not preach. He admitted that he had not found the perfect path, but he did survive, and in time, things did get better.

He also understood and respected my need to do something. He encouraged me to pursue whatever avenues and contacts I could to fight for Thida.

"I had to go to my congressman and fight the Pentagon brass to get what I needed. You do whatever you have to do and know that I support you. I'm proud of you and what you've done. Now you do whatever you have to do to make things right."

My congressman? The idea that Grampi had secured the help of his congressman inspired me. I had seen how everyone at the embassy worked a little harder at crossing the t's and dotting the i's on those cases of "congressional interest." A letter of inquiry from someone in government would be a good strategy to draw attention to Thida's case.

As a Bates student, I immediately thought of Edmund Muskie, the former Maine senator who had just served as President Carter's secretary of state. As the immediate past head of the State Department, his name would have an impact at any US embassy. Muskie was a Bates alumnus and a trustee as well. You use what you have, and this was not a bad card to play at all.

I met with Jim Carrignan, the dean of the college, and related the story of Thida and shared my hope that we might be able to enlist Muskie's support through Bates channels. Dean Carrignan thought the idea sounded reasonable and asked me to draft a brief letter to Muskie that he would then forward under his cover.

The letter was sent.

We waited.

Then, a few weeks later in March, Thida wrote to inform me that Jeff Sandel had come to see her in the camp. A week later, she wrote with news I had been waiting for. She and her family had been interviewed by INS and had been accepted for resettlement in the US. Muskie's office informed me of the same good news through the dean.

After the first wave of refugees was brought to the US directly from Thailand, resettlement agencies observed tremendous challenges in acclimating former rural rice farmers to life in America. In response, the US developed three-month cultural orientation programs in Indonesia and the Philippines to provide English lessons and life skill lessons (how to handle US currency, use Western style toilets, modern kitchen appliances, washers and dryers, etc.) Thida and her family would be among the first refugees to be sent to cultural orientation in the refugee processing center in the Philippines.

By then, Ly and Kolap had arrived in Vancouver, British Columbia and we had connected by phone. We eagerly spoke of reuniting somewhere, but neither I nor they had money. That reunion would have to wait.

31

IMPERFECT REFUGE

Minh Van, the lovely Vietnamese singer who had stolen my not-particularly-well-guarded heart on the beaches of Songkhla, had finally arrived in southern California. We had communicated by telephone and letters since her arrival, and after the initial euphoria of having made it safely to her destination, she seemed to descend into depression, a consequence of her traumatic journey and her separation from her parents and siblings who were still in Vietnam.

I was still single, and I was very moved by her sadness. I naively thought I understood her as well. After all, I had been in the camp with her. I knew the stories of the Vietnamese survivors. I had listened to them as they spoke of their hopes and fears. I knew what she had been through more than others.

She told me she was unhappy living with cousins she hardly knew. She had a menial job in a factory, but the work was tedious. Life in America had not turned out like she had hoped it would.

I repeatedly invited her to move to the East Coast where I would be in a better position to help and support her. There was as much self interest in this plan as there was charity. I had feelings for her. She demurred, saying she might consider it in the future.

THE SCHOOL YEAR ENDED at Bates. I tried, unsuccessfully, to return to Thailand with the International Rescue Committee—they were not at all interested. So, I moved in with my aunt Barbara in her apartment in Hartford. My high school friend, Chris Winsor, had secured a job for me as a machinist at a small machine shop in Collinsville. I worked the overnight shift running aircraft parts on a lathe. I needed money, and the job paid well. I figured I'd get as many hours as I could while I awaited the arrival of Thida and her family.

As the summer wound to a close, following a humbling and monotonous slog of working third shift in a machine shop and spending far too much of my meager earnings in bars with my old high school buddies, I made a quick trip to Orange County to see Minh Van.

I arrived at her apartment to find the living room full of middle-aged Vietnamese men—all suitors for Minh Van, according to one of her friends. Minh Van was not the same person she had been in Songkhla. Her depression had not lifted. She made a weak effort to smile and welcome me, and although I know she appreciated my attention, I had to confront something I always knew was possible but had hoped was not: her interest in me in Thailand had been born of necessity, not attraction. Now, she no longer had to pretend. Now, she no longer had the energy.

The sweet smile, the sparkle, the charm I had been so drawn to in Songkhla were gone. She was distant. Cool.

I was also waking up to the reality that I did not have the wisdom or insight to help her. Working the back channels at the embassy to expedite a deserving compelling case was one thing for an eighteen-year-old to pull off. Helping a deeply injured woman from another culture recover from profound trauma and despair was another. She needed her family and her community. I so wanted to help her. But I was face-to-face with the reality that I was powerless to provide what she needed.

She thanked me for all my help and attention. She confessed that she was in no mind to consider any man, despite ample opportunities.

As we parted, she directly acknowledged my obvious romantic interest in her.

"I know you like me. You like me a lot and you want me to be with you. But I cannot have any man in my life now. You are still too young. You will find another girl. Forget about me."

As I flew home on the red eye from L.A., I wondered. Had I misread all my relationships with my refugee friends? Had Ly and Kolap and Thida merely pretended to be my friends? Would I fault them if they had? I had always understood that there were obvious practical advantages for them in pursuing a friendship with me, but I still wanted so much to believe that what I had felt and experienced was genuine.

Minh Van certainly challenged that notion. Perhaps I had been wrong. Perhaps I had merely been a means to an end for everyone.

BACK IN NEW ENGLAND, my family and I awaited the arrival of Thida and her children. We were nervous, but excited. My parents had coordinated with our church and there were several other families who were at the ready to help Thida and the children once they arrived. The refugee agency in Hartford who had assisted my parents in filing the sponsorship papers back when I was still in Thailand was helping to secure an affordable apartment for the family, who would receive limited funding from the government and agency during their transition period.

But Thida never arrived in Connecticut.

On September 25, 1981, Thida and her children were diverted at the last minute to Long Beach, California.

The change in her destination from Connecticut under my parent's sponsorship to California took us all by surprise. We had received no advance warning.

In one of our first phone calls following her arrival, Thida explained to me that while she was in the Philippines processing center, shortly before leaving for the United States, she had managed to locate her husband's brother in California. As immigration procedures prioritize resettlement with family over that of non-family sponsors, her resettlement destination was automatically changed from Connecticut to California at the very last minute.

It took some time for the news of her diversion to California to sink in. I wanted to feel happy for her, but I could not help feeling a bit disappointed. My family and I had spent a great deal of time and effort planning for her arrival. But mostly, I just missed her. I missed being near her.

But I reminded myself, at least she was finally safe. She seemed to be perfectly happy to end up in California with its growing Cambodian community, kinder weather, and the company of her relatives.

Thida seemed genuinely happy to talk to me. She was safe. She was giddy and spoke so fast I had trouble understanding her.

I was relieved. I looked forward to the day we might meet again. At Christmas 1981, I received a Christmas card from Jeff Sandel.

Dear Scott—

I've been back since October 15th. The JVA bullshit finally won out. They fired my ass. I miss the work terribly and hated like hell to leave.

I tried very hard in the last hectic days to check out your friend THIDA DUONG's case but did not succeed. I'm sure, however, since Mairut was mostly cleared out that she is probably in the US already.

Let me know how you are and what your plans are.

Affectionately,
Jeff

There goes the last of the good guys, I thought to myself. This chapter in my life appeared to be drawing to a close.

I reflected on the whole experience. It still overwhelmed me. I was proud in many ways that I had gone to Thailand, and I was still deeply devoted to my Cambodian friends, but I still couldn't process it all.

What had I accomplished?

Did any of it matter?

CUMBERLAND, RHODE ISLAND, 2000

It would take many years before I would reunite with any of my Cambodian friends again. Of course, we remained in touch by phone and with letters. But in the early years, I was either at college or back in Thailand, where Dennis, who had been promoted to the position of director at the Refugee Section, brought me back every summer and hired me full time after I finished college. Between 1980 and 1985, a period when I began and finished my undergraduate degree, I spent more time in refugee camps in Thailand than I did on my college campus. In those years, we processed over one hundred thousand Cambodians for resettlement in the US—in the same border camps that had been off limits to the embassy when I first arrived in Mairut, including the largest camp, Khao I Dang.

When I returned to the US for good in 1985 to pursue my medical education, I worked in Philadelphia with a refugee resettlement agency, helping many of the same refugees get established in a harsh and often unwelcoming American city.

By the time I moved to Providence, Rhode Island to attend medical school in 1987, Thida had moved to Lowell, Massachusetts, following Kanya, then twenty-five (my age), who was now married to a fellow Cambodian named Narin, and Chanthy, twenty-four, who had married an American named George.

In between medical school rotations, I often visited Thida and her family in Lowell. It is hard to say who enjoyed the visits more—me or Thida. She would often invite her Cambodian friends over when I visited to show me off.

"He speaks Khmer. Go ahead. You can talk to him," she would say to her friends as we sat cross-legged on a mat and ate Cambodian dishes. "He was there, in the camps with us. He knows!"

Again, Cambodians shared their stories of life under the Khmer Rouge and escape to the border. Again, I listened patiently. By now I was accustomed to this ritual and felt comfortable knowing that bearing witness was enough.

I graduated from the Brown University School of Medicine in 1991 and the same year married Emma, my medical school classmate. We stayed in Providence where Emma pursued her residency in family medicine, and I pursued mine in internal medicine with a focus on international health. My plan was to complete my medical training and then return to Southeast Asia along with Emma to continue my work there.

In Providence, while still in medical school, I helped establish a special clinic at a local community health center to serve Cambodians living in Providence. Providence had become home to one of the largest communities of Cambodians in the United States after Lowell, Massachusetts and Long Beach, California.

While I had spent the better part of a decade being groomed for a career in international health, life had other plans for me. In our final week of residency training, our first child, Miles, was born. At birth, Miles was diagnosed with a serious brain malformation. His condition was associated with intractable seizures, quadriplegia, and profound developmental delay.

My international career was no longer feasible given the medical needs of my son. As all parents of special needs children do, we rearranged our lives to better care for him.

For our first jobs after residency training, we moved to the

Mississippi Delta with the US Public Health Service while we simultaneously focused on caring for Miles. For the next few years, preoccupied by demanding work in an underserved medical community combined with multiple hospitalizations and complicated surgeries for my son, I fell out of touch with Thida and her family again. I had fallen out of touch because life had moved on and I had many new demands on my time and attention. But on another level, maybe I needed to take a break from thinking about Cambodia.

But it always came back. Especially the people. On moving back to New England in 1996, I called Thida. But by this time, Thida had moved back to Long Beach, California. Chanthy and her husband George were overseas, doing refugee work. Kanya and her family still lived in Lowell. She had three children with her husband, Narin. He worked for the Massachusetts Department of Labor, and Kanya worked for the Internal Revenue Service. They had done well, and even purchased a home years before I had been able to.

My wife Emma had never met Kanya or any of the others, although she knew their story well. I invited Kanya and her family to visit along with my mother-in-law who was staying with us at the time.

"What did you think of my husband when you first met him?" my wife Emma playfully asked on meeting Kanya.

"I was afraid of him. After he left, I was angry with my mother. 'Why did you bring this American here? What are you trying to do?'"

The evening that had started so well quickly deteriorated.

"I can't believe you abandoned us like that!" She glared at me with eyes that were welling up with tears.

Twenty years had passed since we first met in a small Cambodian border refugee camp. Her emotion was raw.

"I abandoned you?"

Everyone at the table was silent. No one knew what to say or do, least of all me.

"Yes, you abandoned us. I was very, very disappointed with you. I never wanted to see you again." Her voice trembled.

"Kanya. What do you mean I abandoned you? I did everything I could to get you and your family out of that camp!"

My defense fell on deaf ears.

"First, one day, you just left Mairut Camp. Why? Everyone said 'Don't worry. Scott will get us out. He will take care of us.' But you didn't. You said you would sponsor us, but months went by, and we never heard from you. We were supposed to be resettled in Connecticut with you, but we were sent to California to be with my uncle who had nothing!"

Her husband, Narin, gently touched her shoulder.

"It's okay. Listen to Scott. He tried to help you."

I thought of how I had done everything I could with what little resources I possessed to get Thida, her daughter Kanya, and the six other children to safety.

Clearly, Kanya's view of these events was entirely different.

I struggled in the moment to adjust to this unexpected turn. I never had a clue that this was how Kanya felt. When I had visited her in the company of her mother Thida over the years, she played the polite Cambodian daughter, always courteous and welcoming.

Now I saw how hurt she was. As things came into focus, I thought about the "mother-in-law" joke, and wondered if perhaps the joke had gone terribly wrong.

I jumped up from the table and ran upstairs to my office. I pulled out a pack of letters and documents, including every letter her family had ever sent me, letters from the American embassy concerning her family's case, and the original copy of the sponsorship papers. I brought them back to the table and placed them in front of her.

"Kanya, please look. Here is proof I didn't abandon you."

She merely looked down, as if I was not there. She ignored the papers I had placed in front of her.

"Kanya, I didn't abandon you. I never would have abandoned you."

NARIN THANKED US for our hospitality and said perhaps it was time for them to go home.

They departed, and I was left to try to make sense of what had happened. In the days and weeks that followed, I could think of nothing but Kanya's anger and pain. Her emotion had so caught me by surprise. I was stunned and confused. Old feelings of guilt that had been suppressed for twenty years resurfaced, and while I tried to regain my step and return to my routine, I quickly realized I could not move forward without setting things straight with Kanya. I knew I had to apologize for hurting her.

My wife Emma and her mother, who seemed to understand Kanya more clearly than I did, urged restraint.

"Give her some time. Give her some space," they said.

So, I waited. Then, after ten days, having not heard from Kanya, I wrote to her.

September 1, 2000

Dear Kanya—
This is a difficult letter to write, and I don't know where to begin. Well, to begin, I will say I'm sorry.
Kanya, I am deeply sorry, sorrier than you will ever know, to learn how I have hurt you and caused you disappointment, anger and pain. I guess I should have known, but I did not know. I had no idea. You must think I am a fool. Maybe I am. I feel like one.
I want to thank you for finally sharing your feelings with me. I know that took courage for you to come to my house, when you did not want to, and confront me with your words.

I recounted my version of the story and my efforts to get her family off the border. I shared with her that I, too, was deeply disappointed when her family was resettled in California instead of Connecticut with my family.

I am saddened that so many years have passed. But, Kanya, I would feel terrible if you did not want me in your life anymore.
I am hoping you will forgive me. I want my family to get to know you and your family better. Meeting you and your mother was one of the most important things to happen to me in my life.

I hope you are willing to talk with me and see me again. If seeing me brings back too much anger and pain, I will understand. In any event, I pray you find the peace in your heart you deserve.

Sincerely,
Scott

After sending the letter, I waited. Maybe, like it was with Minh Van, it would be better to let go and move on.

A week later, Kanya called.

"I am still angry at you. Seeing you brings back too many bad memories. I had planned to come to your house to confront you, to let you know how you hurt me, and then I planned to never speak to you again.

"But I received your letter. I read it over and over. It made me think. But this is hard for me."

She then shared something with me. As a girl in Cambodia, she had been repeatedly abused. She withdrew from everyone and stopped going to school. She stopped dancing too, which she loved, because she loathed attracting attention to herself. She never told anyone. She said, "I was going to tell my dad before he died," of starvation, under the Khmer Rouge. "But then I said this was not a good thing to tell him before he died. It would only make him sad." In the camps, she and her sisters drew unwanted attention from men who knew the vulnerability of a fatherless family. "When I met you—do you now understand why I was afraid of men?" she asked. "Over time, I realized that you were different than other men. You never looked at me the way other men did. I wrote in my journal that I would want to marry a man like you. My friends started to talk to me. They said, 'Scott is sponsoring your family. He already calls your mom mother-in-law.'

"Then, one day you were gone. My mom said she found my uncle living in California, and we had to go there. In the end, I decided you abandoned us." Thida never told her eldest daughter the full story because that's how the widow led the family after her husband's death. "Mom became more like the traditional Cambodian man," Kanya said. "She would make plans for our family, and she would not always discuss them with us. She would simply tell us what to do."

Kanya and I had both agreed not to tell Thida about our conflict as neither of us wanted to worry her, but she knew.

On a phone call, Thida asked me directly. "When will you be seeing Kanya again?"

"I don't know," I said. "You know she is very busy with her kids and her job."

"Is there a problem with Kanya?" Thida asked.

"Well, no, not really. Kanya is just a little angry with me, that's all."

"Scott. Don't worry. Kanya does not know everything. In those days, I did not discuss everything with her. I know who you are. You are family."

I was comforted by Thida's words. Yet, I would continue to fret.

A week later, I received a thank-you card from Kanya. At the bottom, she wrote, "We would like to visit again."

I called her.

"I will try to see if I can do this," she said.

As she struggled with unearthed memories, Kanya recalled her father's advice to her mother: Keep the family together, no matter what. "I told my mother the other night that I didn't know if I should still talk to you," Kanya told me. "She told me, 'Scott is family. You must keep the family together.'"

Kanya invited us to visit her at her home in Lowell, Massachusetts, about an hour's drive from my home in Cumberland, Rhode Island. She was tentative at first, as her mixed feelings were hard to move past, but she understood we were making a new beginning—not as refugee worker and refugee, but as family. Over the coming months and years, we would make frequent visits to each other's homes, and whenever Thida would come to Massachusetts to visit her children there, we would all get together. In time, after Chanthy returned to Lowell from her work overseas, it became a tradition for us to gather at Chanthy's home the day after Thanksgiving. In time, we were family again.

UNRESOLVED PROBLEMS

After a rough period of readjustment on coming home from the burn hospital, I moved on. I managed fine. Those traumas were behind me. Until they bubbled up again and I dropped everything and confronted my demons and went to Thailand to do what I needed to do. And again, I had a rough period of readjustment on coming home but then moved on. Those traumas were behind me. Until they bubbled up again.

"You may be a doctor, but you need professional help," my wife said in a moment of exasperation after watching how unmoored I had become by Kanya's accusations. Her indictment of me had undermined the house of cards that was my self-image as someone with purpose and moral integrity. My struggle to cope with these old memories began to interfere with my marriage. Emma insisted that I see a psychiatrist.

Although I had survived childhood burns and then immersion in a Cambodian refugee camp, I had never received any professional mental health care. In the early seventies, understanding of child trauma was primitive. The psychiatric profession hadn't even formally recognized the effects of trauma on adults yet. And as I appeared to be functioning well in my day-to-day life, no one had ever suggested that I needed a psychiatrist. Until Emma did. Nearly three decades after I was burned.

She was right. I was not okay.

Dr. Florin was a lovely, quiet man, and he was enormously helpful. I saw him on and off for a few years I think, but Emma says I only went a few times. Whatever it was, it really helped.

I told him of my reunion with Kanya and shared how I was questioning the meaning of it all. He did his best to help me work through my many mixed emotions. We began a dialogue, and with his help, I slowly began to make some order of the trauma and chaos that marked my early years.

Kanya's accusation was just the tip of the iceberg. I had also never fully processed all of the Cambodian accounts of trauma. Earlier in the evening, during the visit where Kanya had confronted me, her husband and I had an opportunity to visit outside as I cooked on the grill. I had never heard Narin's story before, but he was moved to share it.

Narin was a peaceful, dignified man, now nearing the age of fifty. He moved with a gentle authority. "You know," he said, with a soft wariness in his voice, "twenty-five years ago, when I was in my early twenties, at the time of the fall of the Lon Nol government, I remember walking towards my home. From a distance, I heard my mother and sisters wailing.

"The sound of their cries startled me. I ran to my home. I asked my mother 'What happened? What's wrong?' She said, 'They took your father!' My father had been a nurse in the Lon Nol Army. I ran outside. My neighbors said the Khmer Rouge had taken my father and five other men, all soldiers of the Lon Nol Army, out to a field. They said they had shot them. The neighbors told me I had to gather my family and leave before the Khmer Rouge returned. I said I had to go look for my father. They said it is too dangerous—but what could I do? I went out to the field. And there, I came upon my father and five other men from my village lying face down in the field. They were dead. They had been shot—execution style, with one bullet in the back of the head." He shook his head and sighed.

"I returned to my home," he continued. "My neighbors were urging me to take my mother and sisters and leave to another village where my history was not known. They promised me they would bury my father. So, hurriedly, we left."

"Two years later, my mother died—of depression and starvation. Then, two of my sisters died of malaria."

"It got to a point where I just asked 'Okay. So, who will be next?'"

I had heard a thousand stories like it. A thousand deaths. A thousand nightmares. And there, on a peaceful summer evening, as the sun drew near the horizon, in the peaceful sanctuary of a wooded suburban backyard in the security and prosperity of turn-of-the-millennium America, the singular horror of Narin coming upon his father dead in a field in Cambodia shook me.

By sheer coincidence, during this period, Rodney St. Sauveur came back into my life.

I was seeing patients as I did two evenings a week in my colleague's private practice. My day job was as an internal medicine physician at the Rhode Island Department of Corrections, but I maintained a small part-time primary care practice just to keep my community perspective in my field. My partner, Greg Yearwood, and I often consulted each other on cases where a second perspective might be helpful. One evening, I picked up a chart with a note from Greg asking me to see his new patient in consultation for hepatitis C. As a prison doctor where rates of hepatitis C infection were very high, I had treated over one hundred patients and had even published articles on treating the disease in the scholarly literature.

As I lifted the chart from the exam room door, I perused Greg's progress note from his last visit to acquaint myself with the case. "37-year-old man with a history of burns over 85% of his body, treated in 1972 at the Shriner's in Boston." Greg wrote that note simply because that was indeed the story and Greg always included a little story in each of his notes to help him remember the person he was treating. While Greg was well aware of my burns, he would not have known that 1972 was the year I was at the Shriner's.

I opened the door and introduced myself. He said his name was Rodney. He was accompanied by his wife, and they were both quite concerned about the new diagnosis and its implications. After we had chatted a bit about his concerns, I could no longer suppress the urge to ask him a question.

"Do you mind me asking when you were burned?" I asked.

"August 1972."

"You may not have noticed. I also have burns, though not as extensive as yours. Same year. And I was at the Shriner's."

Just then, I had the faint but distinct memory of reading a story to a severely burned seven-year-old boy suspended from wires and pins through his long bones.

"You weren't in the first tent by the left door, were you?"

Thirty-one years after I had read Rodney a story in an attempt to distract him from his pain while he waited for a narcotic to kick in, we were reunited as doctor and patient.

As it turned out, Rodney, with his more extensive injuries, had remained at the Shriner's for well over a year, had returned for multiple surgeries, and, as a result, he still kept in touch with the staff.

"Would you believe that some of the nurses and doctors that took care of us are still there?" he asked. Coincidentally, he had plans to visit the clinic at the Shriner's in a few weeks. "You're free to come along—if you are not too busy."

The Shriner's sat in the same place it did in 1972, but it had been completely rebuilt. Returning to the burn hospital for the first time in decades awoke long buried feelings and emotions. Gone were the fifteen-bed open wards with no windows, now replaced by child friendly rooms with huge bright windows and cheery primary colors. Gone was the constant moaning and tears, pediatric pain control and anesthesia having progressed greatly over the years.

"Oh, we've come so far since you were here," said Michelle Hinson, a nurse who had cared for us years earlier. "We did a lousy job at pain control back then. Pediatric pain control was in the dark ages. And the fact that we had you all in one small dark ward with no windows!"

Still, as I waited in the clinic waiting room while Rodney had his visit with his surgeon, I could not take my eyes off all the little burned children waiting for their appointments. The little blonde girl with long hair and a face deeply disfigured by burns playing with her uninjured sister. The little boy with the missing fingers. The bald teenager in the wheelchair.

The Shriner's Hospital is where I learned that the world is a beautiful place and a horrible place. It is also where I first learned about compassion. Here is where I first learned that I could try to comfort but not to cure.

From a fire to the killing fields, through another world and another culture, and finally, back to the unresolved issue of the fire. I went halfway around the world looking for answers because I couldn't find them in my home. My search, however, ultimately led back to the beginning.

I had left the Shriner's Hospital, but the Shriner's Hospital had never left me. I left the Cambodian border but the Cambodian border would never leave me. I got out of those places, but there are still children on burn wards and there are still refugees fleeing war. There always will be.

When Rodney and I reviewed his risk factors for his hepatitis C, it became clear that his most likely source of infection was the multiple blood transfusions he had received at the Shriner's in Boston in 1972, well before the medical world even knew of the virus.

The treatment for hepatitis C at the time he consulted me over thirty years later consisted of a nine-month course of interferon and ribavirin. It was a difficult treatment with many side effects. The weekly interferon shots made you feel like you had the flu. And in many cases, the treatment failed to eradicate the virus.

Rodney was tough. He never missed an appointment or a dose of his medication. At the end of nine months, we were able to clear the virus. Follow-up blood tests in coming years documented that the virus had been completely eliminated. Working together, we had effectively cured him of a potentially fatal disease that was likely acquired on the ward where we had both been as pediatric burn patients.

It felt good to be able to make that journey with Rodney. I regularly try to help people. I don't always get to succeed.

KIM PHUC

Pat Landau, the mother of my friend Press who had driven me to the bus station that day I left home bound for Thailand, used to ask me "Why did you go to Thailand?"

For me, it seemed obvious.

"Because I was burned, and I felt like I couldn't ignore what was going on there."

"No!" she would shout in growing frustration. "Lots of kids get burned! Lots of kids are traumatized. But they don't run away halfway around the world to refugee camps!"

She had a point. Maybe there was a little more to it. But even I didn't know what it was.

This question was on my mind as I approached my fortieth birthday, shortly after reconnecting with Kanya and meeting up with Rodney, when I happened upon a promotional spot on some cable channel for a documentary about Kim Phuc, the girl in the famous napalm picture from the Vietnam War.

I don't remember who did the documentary, as I only watched it once. I had steeled myself in anticipation of them repeatedly showing "the photo," the naked girl burned by napalm running down the road, the photo that viscerally upsets me to this day. But I hadn't known that in addition to the famous photo, there was also a movie of the event that captured Kim Phuc's horrifying flight down the road towards the camera.

I sat frozen in my chair in front of my TV in the wee hours of the morning and watched Kim Phuc, freshly burned, in shock, run towards me.

Kim Phuc was burned on June 8, 1972. On that day, she was nine and I was ten, living half a world away. Less than two months later, on August 3, 1972, I was burned too.

My sense of connection to her was well established in the months following my own accident. It only deepened as the years went by. My efforts to escape and reinvent myself by traveling halfway around the world were mirrored by her travel to Cuba to pursue her education, something I read about when she was "rediscovered" by the international press in the mid-1980s. Like me, her burns prompted her to pursue a career in medicine. As she began her medical studies in Cuba, I was entering medical school to the north in the United States.

I CELEBRATED MY FORTIETH birthday with my family. Kanya and Chanthy were there with their families. I had explicitly asked for no gifts, having decided instead that I would mark my birthday by making a donation to Kim Phuc's foundation. Along with my check, I sent a brief one-page letter to Kim Phuc. In it, I mentioned the few parallels of our lives, and told her how much I admired her.

Several months later, I was surprised to come home to a voicemail from Kim Phuc telling me that she had only just received my letter. She went on to say it really touched her and she thanked me.

She did leave a number where I could call her. But I never did call her. It would be, I thought, too much.

EIGHT YEARS LATER, in 2010, I happened upon an article online that said Kim Phuc would be speaking at an upcoming meeting of the Burn Survivors of New England to be held at the Florian Hall in

Dorchester near Boston. I immediately knew that I could not pass up the opportunity to sit in the audience and hear her speak. Florian Hall was not so very far from the Shriner's Hospital where I had been treated. It was nearly thirty-eight years since we both had been burned, albeit under very different circumstances.

ALTHOUGH I AM A HEALTH CARE professional and understand how important support groups can be, I had never attended a burn survivors meeting. I suppose I had found other ways to cope and, however dysfunctional those ways might have been, I had managed to get along.

As a doctor, I feel like I am supposed to say that finding myself in a room full of burn survivors filled me with a sense of peace, but it did not. It upset me. I am embarrassed to admit this, but I struggled with nerves from the moment I entered that room.

I do not mean to imply the people themselves upset me. Quite the contrary. These were some of the most wonderful and kind people I could meet. I was warmly welcomed by everyone. As I had come alone, I was quickly spotted and invited to join the very first table as I entered the hall. As fate would have it, it was the table next to the VIP table where Kim Phuc and her family sat.

Among the people at my table were several burn survivors, but the one I remember most clearly is a young teenage woman who happened to come from the Rhode Island town where my medical practice was located and where Rodney lived. She had survived extensive and disfiguring burns involving her head and body and had only recently been discharged from the Shriner's.

"What do you do for work?" she asked me.

"I'm a doctor," I replied.

"Oh. So that's why you're wearing that silly jacket," she said.

I laughed.

The event's speakers were impressive. Iraq War vet Robert Henline, who had been badly burned in an IED attack, disarmed the audience through self-deprecating and endearing humor.

The next speaker, who would be the lead-in to Kim Phuc's keynote, was journalist Fox Butterfield. In college, I had read his book about China, and I was an admirer of his work. Unknown to most of us was the fact that as a young journalist, Fox Butterfield had been in Trang Bang that fateful day in 1972. He was standing next to photographer Nick Ut when Ut took the famous photo of Kim Phuc. Fox Butterfield looked toward Kim Phuc and told the stunned audience that he had never again met Kim Phuc since the day of the napalm strike until this very evening. When he pulled out a small worn notebook into which he had recorded his reporter's notes that day and told the story so familiar to her, even Kim Phuc herself gasped. We were all transfixed.

Then Kim Phuc took to the podium. Now in her mid-forties, the petite woman who had once struggled with the infamy that had been forced upon her now was confident and polished. Smartly dressed and dignified, she was a powerful and gifted public speaker. Rather than be defined by events visited upon her, she had taken control of her life. She explained that she had spent her younger years feeling like she was not in control of her own life. The napalm attack had happened to her. The war had happened to her. The photo and its co-optation as a symbol by so many different people with different agendas had happened to her. But eventually she came to understand that she could leverage her own notoriety to advocate for peace and for compassion for the victims of war. She could take control of her own life and make it what she wanted it to be. She fell in love. She got married. She started a family. And she started a foundation to control her own identity and to pursue the cause of peace on her own terms. Through this process, she found inner peace.

Following her deeply moving speech, the formal program ended. Kim Phuc greeted members of the audience, an audience that was largely made up of burn survivors, Vietnam vets, and a few Gold Star mothers. A spontaneous receiving line formed at her table, the one next to mine.

I did not get in line. Nor did I leave. I could not move. I stood, about ten feet away, frozen, as she graciously greeted and comforted one person after another. Many felt the need to hug her, and she graciously obliged.

After some time, the receiving line had whittled down to about four or five people. At about that time, she noticed me, still standing in the same place. She looked beyond the people in line and squinted to read my name tag. Then she raised her eyebrows as if surprised, and she grabbed the hand of the next person in line and said, "If you'll excuse me for just a moment, I'll be right back."

She walked towards me, and as she came face to face, eye to eye, she said to me "I know who you are."

ABOVE AND TO THE LEFT of my body, I was completely numb.

When Kim Phuc spoke to me I almost fainted. She knew who I was. Do I know who I am? I wondered.

The room hummed with that psychic dissonant noise.

What is happening? What is wrong with me?

After Kim Phuc had finished with the other guests and signing autographs, she returned to me, standing where she had left me, too stunned to move or speak. She told me how much my letter eight years earlier had touched her. She had always hoped we would meet someday. She insisted on giving me an autographed photo of herself and invited me to sit with her husband and children for the reception. I made small talk with her family as she entertained an endless stream of well-wishers, but I quickly felt so exhausted, I could not continue.

I made some excuse about it being late and said goodbye. Kim Phuc scrawled her phone number on a piece of paper and promised we would stay in touch.

I don't know how I made it home, but I watched myself drive the car from where I was. Above and to the left of my body, outside of the moving car. In a daze.

As I entered the house, and my eyes met my wife's, I began to cry.

Emma embraced me.

"I should never have let you go by yourself."

I tried to speak, but I could not. I mean, like I had suffered a stroke, I could not make a sound. I so urgently wanted to tell Emma everything, but I could not make a fucking sound.

It was time to see Dr. Florin again. There was something—I did not know what—that I was still struggling with.

35

THE BOX

I returned to the care of Dr. Florin. In one of my sessions with him, I recalled the childhood toys I had been playing with around the time I was burned. I was burned only two days after my tenth birthday. There were presents I had barely played with. In particular, there were some toy soldiers that I cherished, and I used to keep them on a shelf next to my bed. But I lost them many years ago.

I had a cardboard box that I had packed when I came home from the Shriner's. Every move I had made since I first came home, it came with me. It is my Shriner's box. It has some bandages and splints and get-well cards. I hadn't opened it for many years, but prompted by my session with Dr. Florin, I took the box down.

As I had remembered, there were old rolls of Cling-on, gauze and Xeroform, a few old hand splints, and many get-well cards.

But underneath all that, I found my lost toys. My toy soldiers.

My lost childhood toys had been buried at the bottom of my Shriner's box.

"Well," Dr. Florin commented at our next meeting, "I suppose you don't have to be Sigmund Freud to find some meaning in that!"

Naturally, I shared the story about the burn survivor's meeting, and my reaction to being there and meeting Kim Phuc, how it had all overwhelmed me, and I didn't understand why I could still get so upset after all these years.

"Something happened at the Shriner's," Dr. Florin opined. "Something very different from what happened at the hospital in Connecticut. You've told me about both hospitals, but something in your voice changes whenever we talk about the Shriner's. I want to explore that."

They were both bad, I agreed, but yes, maybe something was different about the Shriner's. I went home and thought on it. The Shriner's was a difficult experience for me. At the Shriner's it wasn't just me who was burned. There were so many other kids, and they were all worse than me. I have carried those memories about the others who were with me ever since.

At our next session, I told Dr. Florin that I had written something about the Shriner's when I was sixteen. Maybe he would like to read it. Maybe he could see something I didn't.

Here is the essay I wrote one year before I left for Thailand:

SANDY

The fluorescent light from the nurse's station across the ward made a dull luster on the cold beige tile floor. On my side, I lay pressed against the chilling smooth metal railing. There was the usual low whir of air through the plastic sterile tents.

It was about two o'clock in the morning. I was on my last hour of Demerol, and I didn't need the clock to tell me that. The fierce itching and hot stinging of my burns kept me awake and conscious.

I was ten years old when I was treated in the intensive care wing of the Shriner's Hospital for severely burned children. Sometimes, however, I think that at this point in my life I had seen and endured more than most people do in their entire lives.

At the time, the Shriner's Burn Institute was at maximum census. Every bed in the East Wing was filled. The atmosphere was one of clutter and confusion.

Off the foot of the bed was the nurse's station. The long counter was a disarray; records and medical supplies heaped in a sort of organized anarchy. To my left were the isolation tents. Constructed from sheets of heavy-duty plastic from floor to low ceiling, these individual tents contained the most severely burned children. The air inside these tents was constantly being changed by the sterile ventilation system. Fortunately, I was not in a tent, but the little two-year-old girl to the left was.

Her name was Sandy. She had fallen into a pot of boiling water, and 98 percent of the surface area of her body was deeply burned.

Struggling with my one functional arm, I set down the railing of my bed and slowly sat up. I felt the usual dizziness while blood and other body fluids trickled down my bare back. Despite orders not to, I grabbed a walker and wrestled myself into a near standing position. My knees, back and arms were all subject to tense muscle contractures, so I crouched like an arthritic old man. Under my bare feet, the floor was cold and hard. With difficulty and discomfort I scuffed and hobbled over to Sandy's bed.

Her lonely eyes pulled me closer to her. She didn't smile; she was no longer able. Occasionally she would twist or writhe pathetically. Her body, once that of a tender infant, now lay shriveled by burns. The silver nitrate had stained portions of her body black. Because the skin had burned off and the scar tissue had been removed, her wounds were exposed. Thick, clumsy bandages weighed down on her tiny weak limbs. They were soaked with her own body fluid drainage. Her body swelled in areas, and her fingers, her tiny baby fingers, were fused together. Sandy lay on wet, stained sheets.

She began to cry again, but her cry only blended with the general cacophony of crying and screaming in the ward. I returned to my bed.

Mary, one of the nurses, had just finished attending to another child and was wheeling the cart over to Sandy's tent. On the cart were packages of Cling-on bandages, Xeroform dressings, and containers of silver nitrate. Mary slipped her newly gloved hands through the envelope opening in the side of the plastic. She was totally covered by a fresh disposable face mask, cap, and apron. I was compelled to watch this ritual as I had many times before.

Mary began whispering calmly and sympathetically. Slowly she began unwrapping the soaked Cling-on that covered Sandy's left foot. She stopped when she reached the thin, red stained gauze wrap around. Being covered by a layer of dried blood, it was hardly discernible. Her foot was puffed and soft.

Up to this point Sandy had been fearfully whining, with an occasional painful scream. I did not know how Mary managed to continue but she did.

Gradually, she began pulling away at the caked bandage. With it came skin, blood, and a cruel piercing scream. My muscles tensed with each scream. I knew that pain well.

This inexorable act was repeated again and again. My hand squeezed tightly on the railing, and my arms and legs began to sting. The screams never subsided until the last bandage had been removed. Sandy lay exposed and wet. Gasping and choking violently, her short painful squeals cut through the random wailing from all parts of the ward. Mary was comforting her.

"It's over, Sandy. It's over."

It was over. The worst part, that is. But Mary was not even halfway through. The sheets had to be changed, the silver nitrate had to be applied, and the wounds redressed. At only two years old, Sandy had to go through this torture once every six hours.

I was thankful that she was through the most painful part.

My fingers loosened up on the bar of my railing, and I lay back on my cool wet sheets.

I still had four hours until it was time for my dressing change. Relieved, I went back to sleep.

"Do you think Sandy's suffering merged with your own suffering?" Dr. Florin asked me. "...That her suffering and your suffering somehow became one?

"And that maybe, after Sandy, you had difficulty looking away from the suffering of others?" he continued. "That somehow your suffering and their suffering are connected?

"My," he said. "What is a ten-year-old boy supposed to do with that?"

EPILOGUE

I eventually did get better at the helping people thing. Of course, I set a low bar with my clumsy efforts at seventeen. Sincerity and good intentions are no substitute for knowledge, skill, and wisdom.

I also continued to heal and learn how to live in this world.

In my adolescence, the idea of a girl and dreams of a comforting intimate relationship helped me cope. I finally graduated from the idea of a girl to true love when I found my wife, Emma, perhaps the only person who really knows, understands, and accepts me with all of my quirks and passions. We have a wonderful, nurturing relationship and are blessed with two amazing children.

I have a respectable career in the field of health and human rights, and I care for patients with developmental disabilities in a medical practice inspired by our son Miles that Emma and I founded over a decade ago.

So, for the most part, I am happy. I'm damaged goods, but I'm happy.

Thida and I remained close, and I was at her bedside in a hospital in Long Beach in 2004 when she died from a massive stroke at the young age of fifty-eight. By the time I arrived at the hospital, she was unconscious and on life support. I took my turn sitting alone with her during the final vigil to allow her children a break. In her final hours, I grasped her hand as tightly as she had held mine the day we met in a squalid border refugee camp twenty-four years earlier. This time, it was me who had trouble letting go.

Thida did have a good life in the US, but there were many ups and downs. She did find a new home as part of the Long Beach, California Cambodian community where I had the opportunity to visit her many times over the years. She supported herself doing piecework as a seamstress working from her house where she was also raising her children, and later her grandchildren. But she did not entirely escape further trauma and violence. A few years after arriving in Long Beach, her son Vongsa was killed in the crossfire of a gang-related shooting. Vongsa was not involved in a gang, but gangs flourished in the early days of the newly immigrated Cambodians, Vietnamese, and Laotians, and he was standing on the wrong street at the wrong time. Another son, Rasmey, did join a gang. He would eventually serve time in prison, and years after his mother passed, he would die too, in a single car accident in Nevada. But the remaining six children all did well, secured good jobs, had children of their own. They moved forward with new lives in America. And in her final years, Thida never lost her ability to enjoy her children, her grandchildren, her many friends in the Cambodian community, and our enduring friendship.

Still, the burden of trauma is physical as well as emotional. It is cumulative and it is lifelong. I have no doubt that Thida's early stroke was due in part to everything she had experienced in the war, under the Khmer Rouge, as a refugee, and as an immigrant in a new and strange country.

Similarly, the childhood trauma of my own accident and the suffering of the burn ward, compounded by front row exposure to the horror of the Cambodian holocaust while I was still very young, continue to haunt me. The echoes of childhood injury return to my consciousness and disrupt my world at a moment's notice—even after periods lasting years where I have lived in relative peace and stability. Years where I begin to believe I have healed more or less, even if imperfectly. But I will never completely escape the mark of my accident and the aftermath. There is no cure. But like the physical scars I bear, I have learned to live with those things I cannot change. Like the undisguised truth about this world. That it is harsh. That it is cruel. That pain is unavoidable. That children will suffer.

But also, that one can still find joy and meaning in this world by seeing, acknowledging, and responding to the suffering of others. And that, whatever one believes about restorative justice in the afterlife, we can get through *this* life now through human connection, humor, compassion—love actualized by helping others.

I still think of Thida as the angel that saved my soul and allowed me to move forward on my journey towards healing. When I met her, I was so close to giving up on this world. I did not want to be a part of it because I couldn't find joy, happiness, or meaning in a world so filled with sorrow. I had figured out how to get up each day, how to go to school, how to present myself as emotionally intact even though inside I wasn't. I had modeled myself after the older men I knew who had survived great adversity and appeared intact—my grandfather, my burn surgeon, the fire chief. But something critical was missing.

How do I put the pieces of a shattered life back together into something that resembled a life I would want to live? In the early years after coming home from the hospital, I cobbled together primitive strategies to cope, to survive. They call that resilience. I hate that word. I wish children never had to be resilient. I wish we could protect them from trauma instead. Of course, we can't always do that. In any case I was not satisfied with resilience. To be resilient is to endure. I wanted to do more than endure. I wanted to figure out the puzzle. I wanted to live and thrive in this world. And I felt a need to respond and connect to the suffering of others—without being consumed by it—but I did not know how to actually do it.

Thida showed me how to live and blossom in a cruel world. She did it simply by existing, by being Thida, by showing me how to laugh and love in the aftermath of utter horror. She boldly took the initiative to make a connection with me. She believed in me and never doubted me. Her faith in me helped me believe in myself. She had faith that I would be able to help her and others, and in the long run, she was right. I could help and ultimately, I did help. She modeled compassion for others, including the genuine love and compassion she showed to me through our enduring friendship. Through her I was able to learn how to meaningfully channel the compassion I felt for the suffering of others. In truth, I learned this lesson through Ly and Kolap and many of the refugees I knew and would come to know over the ensuing decades (as well as from my many patients). But she was the one who first took my hand and started to walk with me on my path to healing.

The still broken young man who largely failed on his first attempt to meaningfully help suffering Cambodians and left Thailand battered, bruised, and exhausted, returned within two years to complete three more tours with the US Embassy Refugee Program. That ever so slightly more competent young man helped a small US team of embassy caseworkers successfully process refugees off the border by the thousands.

Having dropped out of high school, I resumed and completed my formal education, becoming a physician, and later, a human rights activist. I took on and fought for many worthy causes and, while I would often fail, I found meaning in seeing and caring about people others didn't see. I found meaning in highlighting injustice in places others ignored, and in fighting to help wherever I could—whether I had a chance of succeeding or not.

Thida was a fighter. She was a fighter who used love, humor, and compassion to find meaning and purpose in a cold world. On her arrival to the Thai border, she stared down the Thai soldiers with their M-16 rifles pointed at her. When they threatened to shoot her, she said "Then shoot me. We are not going back."

We are not going back. We are going forward.

I have tried to be like her, not because I am a good or generous person by nature, but because her example is the only one that let me move forward. Her example has guided my life and work to a path that facilitated healing.

I refused to give up on my relationship with Kanya. Eventually, we worked through our difficulties to the best of our abilities. Our families remain close, and our lives have stayed very much intertwined. Thida's extended family—now including grandchildren and great-grandchildren—accept me as a respected family elder. Imagine that. For the many years we lived near each other on the East Coast, our families would get together throughout the year, including every year the day after Thanksgiving. Emma and I took one of her granddaughters into our home for a year when she required protection as a vulnerable child witness to a gang shooting. Since I moved to California in 2011, Kanya, Chanthy, Tevy, and Malis have visited me often. And in between, phone calls, text messages, and social media exchanges keep us connected. Thida's family is my family.

Ly and Kolap remain among my dearest and most special friends and are also my family. They had succeeded in their effort to be resettled in a third country, Canada, but it took over a decade before they would be reunited with their children. The children were fully grown when they finally met their parents again.

After nearly two decades in Canada, Ly and Kolap returned to Cambodia to live. Kolap would later tell me that even after twenty years she never stopped feeling like a refugee there. When I was finally able to visit Cambodia for the first time in 2001, they met me at the airport as they had promised me they would all those years ago in Mairut Camp. It had taken twenty-one years for us to reunite, but I have been back to visit them several times since then. Ly still has the wire cutters I smuggled into the camp after the artillery attack. He says they remind him of his hard-fought freedom and our friendship. Plus, they come in handy around the house.

In 2022, in preparation for the completion of this book, I looked for and found Minh Van through an internet search. I sent a letter with an old picture of us together to the address. Three days later, I received a text. "OMG. I can't believe you found me." She was happy to reconnect. Only a few months after I had parted ways with her, her life turned for the better when she met a successful Vietnamese music producer who had arrived in the US in the first evacuation during the fall of Saigon in 1975 and was well established in California. He too was charmed by Minh Van's singing. They were married a few months later. Today, they have been happily married for forty years and have two adult children and now grandchildren. Soon after reconnecting, our families met at the Vietnamese restaurant she and her husband owned in Little Saigon, Orange County. I had worried about her for years. I was relieved to see that she had prospered.

Dennis Grace would remain with the embassy until 1995, and after overseeing the resettlement of five hundred thousand refugees, he returned to the states to serve in the Bush Administration as the deputy director of the Office of Faith-Based and Community Initiatives. The opportunities Dennis gave me as a young man were the foundation of my entire professional career, and we remain friends.

Following his treatment for hepatitis, Rodney and I became friends, and I continued to be his physician and he my house painter until I moved west. His story, including his medical history, is used with his gracious permission. Rodney's optimism and tenacity continue to inspire me.

Jody Nolan, my Shriner's buddy who was the sole survivor of the camping fire that took the lives of his father and three siblings, died at age forty-six from cancer before I could ever find him again as an adult. Since learning of his death through an internet search, I have made donations to Shriner's Hospital in his memory.

Maureen, the girl who I adored as a child, remains a good friend. She, too, felt a call to help others and became a nurse.

In 1979, photojournalist Susan Meiselas took the photo of the stunned children moments after they were injured by a bomb in Nicaragua. That was the picture that I described in my first letter to my parents as the picture that finally put me over the edge and set me on my determined path to join the Cambodians on the Thai border. In 2019, I was the co-recipient of an award for work that colleagues and I had done as physicians advocating for vulnerable children on the US border. Susan is on the board of the Ridenhour Foundation (named for Ron Ridenhour who first reported the story of the My Lai massacre in the Vietnam War) which gave the award. I was eventually able to meet Susan in her New York studio and share my story of how her photo had impacted my life.

As I prepared the final version of this memoir, I impulsively made a short visit to see Ly and Kolap in Cambodia on the occasion of my sixtieth birthday in the summer of 2022. The COVID pandemic had prevented me from traveling for a few years, and I felt an acute need for their presence—exactly fifty years after my life was changed by a gasoline tank explosion. I felt the need to sit with them to be re-centered by their love and wisdom. Although the visit was short, it was rich. We reflected on everything that had happened since we first met in a refugee camp forty-two years earlier. We sat together on the porch of their daughter's home in Phnom Penh, Ly shirtless as he often was in the camp. He and Kolap live a simple life in Cambodia, forswearing the consumer-based wealth absorbed lifestyle they had encountered not only in the West, but increasingly at home in Cambodia.

"Know when you have enough. When you have enough, stop," Ly said.

Kolap, ever mystical and insightful, looked at me with concern in her eyes.

"Scott, you worry too much. You worry about your son, you worry about refugees, people who are sick. Enough. It's enough. You have done enough. It's time for you to rest."

On the way home, I thought about Kolap's advice. I hadn't even spoken about things that worried me during our visit, but she knew. Four decades later, Ly and Kolap still have wisdom to impart and are still teaching me how to move forward on my journey. I know Kolap is correct.

But I am left, always, with the stories.

While listening to survival stories of Cambodians overwhelmed me as a teenager, I have grown more comfortable through the passing years with listening to those stories. They still horrify me. They still haunt me. But, nowadays, when a survivor of the Cambodian killing fields learns that I was in the camps, they often feel they can trust me. That ability to listen I first developed on the Cambodian border helped me in my work as a physician as well. People who are suffering need to be seen and heard.

Before I departed from Cambodia, I visited a Cambodian doctor friend who I had collaborated with when I was on the faculty at Brown University and in cofounding a nonprofit agency to help poor rural Cambodians. Even though I had heard the essence of her story before, in a quiet moment, she shared her deeply personal story of survival during the war and the Khmer Rouge period more completely. Her village had been heavily bombed by the Americans, and then under the Khmer Rouge she was sent far from her family as part of a youth group. Her brother died in the war. Her father was imprisoned and tortured. As she began to tell her story, her son, a sweet and thoughtful young man who had just graduated from college in the US, politely excused himself as his mom started telling a tale he had undoubtedly heard parts of many times before.

She watched him leave the room, then looked directly at me.

"It's okay," she said. "I can tell you—because you understand."

Seeing and acknowledging other people's suffering matters.

Ultimately, we will not end suffering. Even in my callow youth, I understood that noble truth. But connecting with people, seeing them, hearing them, acknowledging them, comforting them, and joining together with them on the communal journey of shared human experience that inevitably involves suffering matters. The simple and often imperfect acts of compassion we do for others matter. In the end, I have come to believe compassion may be the only thing that matters.

ACKNOWLEDGEMENTS

This book results from an on-and-off effort that spanned two decades. I am grateful for the seemingly limitless patience, love, and encouragement provided by my wife, Emma. I could not have sorted out my story without her help. This account doesn't come close to capturing all that she endured throughout the long journey.

No one can read this story and not feel for my parents. Their son nearly killed himself in his backyard in a fiery accident, underwent a lengthy hospitalization and recovery, and then ran away to a war zone. Through it all, their love, support, and faith in me were unwavering.

While Thida's spirit was the light, my wife and my parents were the rock on which my recovery was built.

Many individuals helped along the way, but two stand out as the true believers of a project I often abandoned: Evan Howard and Jody Rich. Many years ago, Evan invited me to join his writer's group at Community Church in Providence, Rhode Island. Along with Evan, group members A.D. Van Nostrand, Joan Pettigrew, and Dick Upson reviewed a first draft in early 2001. With their support, I completed a first draft later that year. That version was unfocused and unwieldy, and yet *Bates Magazine* editor Jay Burns managed to extract and publish an excerpt. And then I put it away. For the next two decades, Evan and Jody continued to periodically and persistently nudge me to return to the long fallow project. In 2021, I yielded, and with the help of Evan, Jody, and editor Susan Leon, I completed the manuscript in 2023.

Marty Duckenfield and Evan Howard provided helpful feedback on final revisions. Barbara Braman generously provided the cover for artwork. Steven and Dawn Porter of Stillwater River Publications provided a publishing platform. Fellow burn survivors Rodney St. Sauveur, George Pessotti of the Burn Survivors of New England, and the amazing Kim Phuc provided encouragement and inspiration along the way.

Conspicuously absent from this version of the story is the off-screen role played by Ed Powers' wife, Andrea Fowler. Andrea also worked for the embassy, and her portfolio included "unaccompanied minors." Rick Barnes probably never intended to hire me at the embassy, but Andrea, who had seen me from afar in Mairut on a scouting visit, lobbied on my behalf. "Let's give him a chance. He's out there on his own and if we don't take him under our wing, he's going to get himself killed." I only learned that critical detail decades later, and it helps make sense of the most unlikely part of the story—how a seventeen-year-old got hired by a US embassy. While the manuscript preserves the story as I lived and experienced it, the impact of her behind-the-scenes kindness should not go uncredited.

Obviously, the above list is incomplete. Over the years, many friends, family, and acquaintances have shown interest in this story and encouraged me. My father's prophecy proved true: "For the rest of your life, you will have to explain what you did and why you did it to everyone who asks."

So, thank you to everyone who asked along the way. You helped shape this story.

Photo by Jocelyn Haubert

Dr. Scott A. Allen is a physician and professor emeritus at the University of California, Riverside. He is internationally recognized in the field of health and human rights, most recently for helping bring attention to the conditions of children in US immigration detention, work for which he and his colleagues received a 2019 Ridenhour Prize and the Physicians for Human Rights Award. He is the co-founder of the Center for Health and Justice Transformation and founder and medical director of The Access Clinic, a primary care practice for adults with intellectual and developmental disabilities located in Riverside county in southern California where he lives.

More information is available at www.drscottallen.com.

www.ingramcontent.com/pod-product-compliance
Lightning Source LLC
Chambersburg PA
CBHW060501090426
42735CB00011B/2063